MANAGING YOUR EMOTIONS

MANAGING YOUR EMOTIONS

Erwin Lutzer

CHRISTIAN HERALD BOOKS
Chappaqua, New York

All Scripture quotations, except those noted otherwise, are from the *New American Standard Bible*, © 1960, 1962, 1963, 1968, 1971, 1972, 1973, 1975, and 1977 by The Lockman Foundation, and are used by permission.

Library of Congress Cataloging in Publication Data

Lutzer, Erwin, W.
    Managing your emotions.

        1. Christian life—1960-   2. Emotions.
I. Title.
BV4501.2.L89   248.4   80-69311
ISBN 0-915684-81-0   AACR1

MEMBER OF
EVANGELICAL CHRISTIAN
PUBLISHERS ASSOCIATION

Christian Herald, independent, evangelical and interdenominational, is dedicated to publishing wholesome, inspirational and religious books for Christian families.

First Edition
CHRISTIAN HERALD BOOKS, 40 Overlook Drive, Chappaqua, New York 10514
Printed in the United States of America

To the memory of my nephew, Dallas, whose untimely death introduced us to the emotion of sorrow.

Contents

Preface

GOD CREATED us with emotions so that we might be able to enjoy Him and His creation. Often we have been tempted to consider our feelings as a bother, a hindrance to living a life of faith. Although it is true that as fallen creatures our emotions often lead us astray, we must remember that God gave us emotions so that we might live a well-balanced and wholesome life. After all, God Himself is an emotional Being who expresses anger, pleasure, and compassion. Our goal, then, ought not to be to suppress our emotions but rather to achieve emotional wholeness through finding God's answers for our emotional needs. If those who read this book should be helped along the road to emotional stability, my efforts will be well rewarded.

I'm indebted to many people who have helped shape my thinking about emotion: Jay Adams, James Dobson, and David Augsburger come immediately to mind. Also, I'd like to express a special word of appreciation to my pastor, Richard Sipley, for his provocative thoughts regarding the problems of human emotions. His insights are particularly reflected in my chapters on love and fear.

I wish to thank my good friend, Mr. Les Stobbe, for his encouragement and editorial assistance. And I am especially appreciative of my secretary, Terri Ambrula-vich, who typed the manuscript. Finally, I am grateful to the people of the Moody Church, who have given me the privilege of sharing the fruits of my study with them.

Erwin W. Lutzer

1

Learning to Cope

EMOTIONS. What should we do with them?

Although some might feel that God was rather stingy in bestowing some of His gifts, we would all agree that He was generous when He gave us emotions. We all have experienced so many passions and feelings that, as one person has correctly said, we are millionaires in emotions—they come in infinite combinations of type and intensity. Just as we may experience physical pain or pleasure, so we have the capacity to experience emotional pain or pleasure. Feelings are an indispensable part of our humanity.

Unfortunately, we usually think of our feelings in negative terms. We're so accustomed to hearing the phrase "emotional problems" that we think our emotions are a bother, a liability. No doubt many of us have thought at some time that we'd be better off without them.

As a result, many of us try to ignore our emotions. This seems to be a popular approach taken by many Christian writers who see our emotional makeup as a hindrance to progress in the Christian life. We've had the impression that our emotions are an embarrassment to us, an unwanted appendage.

For example, we're all acquainted with the fact, faith,

11

and feeling trilogy. We are told that our forgiveness is based on facts, namely, the death and resurrection of Jesus Christ. We must exercise faith in these facts, and then our feelings will eventually follow suit. At any rate, our feelings must be ignored; they are a hindrance to a life of pure faith.

I happen to agree with this analysis, at least to some extent. Yes, feelings do lead us astray; yes, we must believe the facts of the gospel, regardless of the emotional turbulence we may experience. But are our emotions simply an appendage, an enemy of Christian growth and maturity?

To say that we should believe facts and ignore feelings is to invite people to deny their feelings, to encourage them to suppress their negative emotions rather than benefit from those emotions. Husbands often have developed insensitivity toward their wives by simply repeating what they have heard in church, namely, that your feelings should be rejected. Yet those feelings are important. They are a part of our total being.

I've known angry people who deny their anger; they simply are unable to admit such feelings, believing that that would be tantamount to a confession of spiritual carnality (that such is not the case will be seen in the chapter on anger). Others deny hostility, bitterness, or sorrow. Thinking that Christians should not have such feelings, they insist that they are free from them. The result is that deep feelings often smolder beneath the surface of their personalities. I am convinced that emotional wholeness cannot be achieved through denying the deep emotions that we all have from time to time.

Some have allowed the pendulum to swing in the opposite direction. They have made their feelings the focus of their attention. Our nation has become steeped in sensuality (i.e., the belief that we should be motivated by our senses). Watch the ads on television and you'll soon learn that we have placed a high priority on "feeling just right." There is a drug for virtually every physical pain, every emotional disturbance. If you feel down, take "uppers"; if you're emotionally excitable, take "downers." But at all costs, feel good.

Much of modern psychology has contributed to this focus of our pleasure-seeking generation. For one thing, modern man believes he has evolved from lower forms of life, which means he is made up solely of *matter*—he has no immaterial substance, such as a soul or a spirit. Therefore, all human feelings are only physical or chemical reactions. The conclusion is that all emotional disorders have a chemical cause. Since nothing can ever be wrong with me spiritually, there can only be physical disorders, and these can be cured with drugs.

Also, modern psychology, cut loose from moral absolutes, is incapable of judging behavior. Thus, we can understand why people would conclude that they can do whatever they feel like doing. If you have a sexual urge, fulfill it; if you have anger, express it; if you feel tied down, walk away from your responsibilities. At any rate, it's your life and you're number one, so do as you please. The bumper sticker says it all: "If it feels good, do it!"

I would remind you that following your feelings, doing whatever your animal urges dictate, is the surest way to a life of spiritual ruin. All of us were born with a sinful nature that wants to have its desires fulfilled. And although our feelings in themselves may not be sinful, fulfilling them without the instruction of Scripture and the power of the Holy Spirit would be disastrous. Michael Quoist has said, "Emotions and physical desires are like head-strong steeds . . . . you have to keep the reins firmly in hand." Blindly following your feelings is assuredly not the path to happiness.

Between these two extremes lies the biblical balance that we must proclaim to this emotionally distraught generation. This necessitates the following affirmations.

1. *God the Creator has emotions and therefore endowed us, who are created in His image, with a similar emotional capacity.* Throughout the history of the church, theologians, and particularly philosophers, have denied that God has feelings. Apparently, it was believed that such an admission would demean the concept of an immutable God. For instance, the Westminster confession of faith states, "There is but one only living and true God who is . . . without body, parts or *passions*" (italics mine, II 1, 1648). But the Scriptures teach otherwise: "And the LORD was sorry that He had made man on the earth, and He was grieved in His heart" (Gen. 6:6). God became weary of hypocrisy (Isa. 1:11-14), and of course His anger against sin is expressed numerous times throughout the Bible.

Look at Christ, who displayed the divine nature. He expressed sorrow (John 11:35), anger (Mark 3:5), frustration (Luke 9:41), amazement (Luke 7:9), and joy (Heb. 12:2). Thus, to deny our emotions, to be unwilling to admit our anger, is to be unprepared to do what God Himself does, namely, to affirm that He is indeed angry with the wicked. Our emotional makeup is but one of the ways by which the image of God is seen in us.

2. *Man created in the image of God is a physical, spiritual, and emotional unity.* With our bodies we can relate to our physical environment, with our spirits we can be in fellowship with God, and with our emotions we can be affected by either relationship. In fact, we sometimes cannot easily separate the various aspects of man in common experience. When we act or react to circum-

stances, we are intricate, unified, and mysterious beings. As a result, our emotions can be affected by our relationship with God or the haphazard and fluctuating experiences of life.

One day a two-year-old child wanders away from home and is lost for several hours. The parents, neighbors, and police search frantically but without result. Two other children were kidnapped in the area within the last year. The child's parents are filled with regret ("Why did we let him play alone in the front yard?"), anger ("Who would do such an awful thing?"), and fear ("How can we cope in the days ahead?"). But just before sundown, the child is found sleeping peacefully in a neighbor's garden. Imagine the elation when the parents discovered that all their turbulent emotions were unfounded. Think of the relief, satisfaction, and joy when the boy has his supper and is tucked into bed that evening.

Now visualize an entirely different scene. A woman filled with depression has already put the sleeping pills in her purse. This will be her last day on earth. But before she swallows the contents of that small jar, she decides to make one last stop at a friend's house; it will be her way of saying good-bye. To her surprise, she finds several women gathered in the home for, of all things, a Bible study. The depressed woman is invited to stay, and she does so reluctantly, thinking this will be her last time to give God—if He exists—a chance. After the study, the despondent woman lingers to ask some questions: "Can God do something for me?" An hour later, she realizes that it was the guilt from an ongoing illicit sexual relationship she was having that was the cause of the depression. She accepts Christ's forgiveness for her sin, and suddenly the heavy sense of guilt and depression is gone. The bottle of pills lies unopened in her purse as she leaves for home, light-hearted, free, and clean.

These true stories remind us that our emotions can be deeply affected by either our circumstances or our relationship with God. Physical illness affects our emotional equilibrium. And the reverse is also true: our emotions can affect our bodily health. Many diseases are considered psychosomatic; the physical ailment is caused by emotional disorders. We cannot live with guilt, for example, without having it affect our body. Anger exacts an enormous physical penalty—it can cause everything from ulcers to backaches. I read recently that heart attacks are more often caused by emotional stress than lack of exercise. The consequences of emotional disorders are built right into the basic fabric of human life. We can talk about our body, soul, and spirit for the purpose of analysis, but we live, breathe, and react as one entity, a unity.

3. *God created us with emotions so that our lives might be enriched.* God could have created us without emotions; we could be intelligent, calculating, insensitive machines. But life would be exceedingly dull. True, there would be no sorrow, but there would be no joy, either. We would live without a sense of anticipation, and we would not experience the comfort that can be ours at a time of tragedy. Life would progress without the laughter of children, without the spontaneity of lovers or the sympathy of friends. But we've learned that God is not like that, nor did He wish us to be. Our emotions were given not to control us, but that we might be able to enjoy life. We would *not* be better off if we were free of them.

4. *God's primary means of bringing about our emotional healing is by working through our spirit rather than adjusting our physical or environmental circumstances. Consequently,*

our negative emotions such as bitterness, rejection, and anger are not to be ignored. Just as bodily pain is God's way of telling us that something has gone awry with our physical nature, so emotional pain may tell us that all is not well with our spiritual nature. And if we try to solve a spiritual problem with a physical remedy (such as curing depression with drugs), the results will be disappointing.

It's popular to think that the answer to our spiritual need is a physical stimulus. In a shopping mall, I overheard a sales clerk say to a customer, "You owe it to yourself to get these cosmetics. All of us are in the dumps once in a while, and we deserve to make ourselves happy. If the people around you don't make you happy, then it's up to you to make yourself happy." If a customer accepted this advice and did indeed feel better because of her improved appearance, she would be greatly mistaken to interpret that improvement as the answer to life's doldrums. A physical remedy can at times appear to solve a spiritual problem, but it can only camouflage the real source of the trouble. Our spiritual and emotional natures must ultimately be brought into harmony with God. Only then can we achieve emotional balance. Remember Augustine's words: "O Lord, Thou hast made us for Thyself and our hearts are restless until they find their all in Thee."

I'm not saying that all emotional disorders have a spiritual cause. Our physical condition can affect our emotional stability; drugs can cause emotional disturbances that can be either detrimental or beneficial. But God's desire for each person is emotional and spiritual wholeness; *He wants our emotional stability to be based on our relationship with Him rather than on physical or chemical stimuli.*

What, then, should we do with our emotions? The

answer is to (1) admit to ourselves and to God how we feel (sometimes we should admit our feelings to others, too) and (2) ask ourselves: Why do I feel the way I do? (The answer to this question is often difficult and sometimes impossible to give. We've all felt like David, who asked himself, "Why are you in despair, O my soul? And why have you become disturbed within me?" [Psalm 42:5a]). But more importantly, we must (3) find out what the Bible teaches about this particular emotion so that we will have divine direction on managing those fluctuating feelings that we all experience.

Then, (4) we must realize that emotional wholeness follows obedience and not vice-versa. Many people do not obey God's Word because they think they must feel like it; that is, they think that unless they obey with emotional exhilaration, they are guilty of hypocrisy.

Not true. No doubt Christ did not feel like going to the cross; the thought did not give Him emotional pleasure. Yet in the end He experienced the emotional satisfaction of joy (Heb. 12:2). The joy followed obedience, it did not precede it.

Suggested Application

1. Write down all the emotions you have experienced within the past week. Can you remember what caused the fluctuation in those feelings? Circumstances? Your relationship with God? Your health?

2. Read the gospels, looking for clues regarding the emotions Christ felt when He was here on earth. Here are a few passages to get you started: Matthew 9:36; 26:36-46; 27:46; Mark 3:5; Luke 24:25; John 11:35; 12:27-28.

3. Study the nine aspects of the fruit of the Spirit (Gal. 5:22-23), and highlight those that directly influence our emotions.

4. Discuss: In what ways do we often deny our emotions—or suppress them rather than facing them and then doing something about them?

5. God expects us to have a feeling of compassion. What sins dull our sensitivity to human need (see Eph. 4:17-24)?

6. What emotions do you want God to help you control in your life? List ways to face those feelings so that they might be made subject to Christ.

2

Steps to
Emotional Wholeness

WHILE driving from Dallas to Chicago, my wife and I stopped at a restaurant for dinner. Moments later, a woman and her three-year-old daughter came and sat at the table next to us. We exchanged pleasantries, and our own children spoke with the little girl, who sat close to her mother.

Fifteen minutes later, a man walked in and sat beside the woman, and a conversation ensued. From bits and pieces of the discussion, we put the story together: they'd been divorced and had agreed to meet here to transfer their daughter from one to the other. The little girl listened as her parents talked and argued in her presence. They disagreed regarding the amount of money that had been paid for alimony, and the matter was left unresolved. Then the father left with his daughter walking beside him. She waved good-bye to her mother, and together they walked into the night.

Think of what this three-year-old girl faces: she is to love her mommy during the week and her daddy on weekends. But her mommy and daddy don't love each other: no, they can't be together for five minutes without an argument. She's supposed to feel secure even though her daddy has found someone more exciting than her mommy to live with. She'll have to adjust to her "new" mommy, too. Meanwhile, she is transferred from one to the other like a package; she doubtless thinks she is a bother, a nuisance to these adults who gave her physical life.

This girl represents millions of children who are either unloved or think they are unloved because of the breakup of the family. More than one-half of all the children born today will, at some time, live with a single parent. Add to this the estimated two million children who are physically abused and we readily see that the emotional consequences are immense. We are already reaping the harvest—millions of people experience depression, rejection, frustration, and guilt. Yet, I think we've seen only the tip of an iceberg; the consequences will escalate from generation to generation.

What is the answer? Many Christians believe that we need the techniques of psychiatry to help those who can no longer cope with their emotional handicaps. Without entering the current debate regarding the extent (if any) to which psychiatry and Christianity can be harmonized, let me say that it is indeed doubtful whether we can integrate a secular approach with a biblical one. I've found that the message of the Bible is almost always diluted when we seek help from secular sources. Even the argument that we can profit from the analysis of psychiatry and apply a biblical solution, in my opinion, fails. The Bible is God's revelation, and as He is the Creator, He alone knows the answer to the deepest human needs. One reason we have often turned to secular psychiatrists for help is that we have ignored biblical guidelines. Because we don't have time to become involved in people's lives, we'd prefer to have someone else deal with those who are emotionally crippled.

At the risk of over-simplification, let me suggest some basic steps needed in emotional healing. I'm not saying that their application is simple; in most instances, it takes time to overcome the hurts of the past. But I believe that God has not left us without resources in our quest for emotional wholeness. Christ is well able to heal the brokenhearted.

1. *The past must be forgiven by God, and we must be cleansed from its influence.* Later I shall explain more fully the need for both forgiveness and cleansing. At this point let's define the difference. Forgiveness is God's gift to us that assures us of a right standing in His presence. Cleansing is the application of forgiveness to us directly. It is important that the past be put behind us, both legally and in experience.

Some people speak about the need for the healing of memories. My wife attended a session with a person who had a woman from the audience recount in detail her sexual experience with her grandfather. The purpose was that this woman might be able to think of Christ during the experience and put the emotional trauma of that event behind her. Although I can appreciate the goal of such therapy, I question its biblical validity.

There is an emphasis in the Scriptures, however, on the renewing of the mind. I believe that God is able to heal our memories. That does not mean that we will never think of the unpleasant experiences of the past, but they need not become the focus of our attention. I've spoken to people who can recall only with great difficulty some of the crushing experiences they had because God has renewed their minds. The present and the future occupy their attention, and their past no longer has control over them.

The apostle Paul alluded to this in Ephesians 4, where he told us that many people have given themselves over to sensuality and impurity. Then he talked about our life without God, the corruption and the control of lusts that are latent within us all. But then he urged us to be "renewed in the spirit of your mind, and put on the new self, which in the likeness of God has been created in righteousness and holiness of the truth" (vv. 23-24). The renewed mind is different from the natural mind, which focuses on negative emotions rather than the positive light of the gospel.

We all know it is God's will that Christ be formed in us, that we be changed into His likeness. We are to be "conformed to the image of His Son." Surely, therefore, God does not want us to be chained to the hurts of the past, as such enslavement would hinder Christ-likeness. He forgives us and then cleanses our minds from the ill effects of the rejection and guilt that we may carry with us. I'm not saying that such deliverance will take place speedily, although I have known those who have had instant deliverance from the harassment of past memories. But if we stand our ground, there will be emotional release.

More specifically, the blotting out of our past necessitates clarifying erroneous concepts. For example, many people have wrong notions of God that make them afraid of Him rather than perceiving Him as a God of acceptance and love. So a foundation must be laid to help people with destructive emotions. Or consider those who have grown up in homes in which sex was considered sinful even within prescribed biblical limits. Such a person may grow up and marry, only to learn that he or she cannot relate sexually to a marriage partner. Here again there must be clarification that will enable the person to be freed from childhood inhibitions. The cleansing we have talked about must take place within the context of biblical teaching so that the mind can be filled with God's perspective.

Future chapters will discuss in detail the need to for-give those who have wronged us. So let me state simply that only when we choose to forgive those who have wronged us can we expect that the bitterness and the emotional hurt will begin to subside. Forgiveness is something we do for others, but we also do it for our own good. It's part of the process of wiping out a hurt-ful past.

2. *We must exalt the cross as God's answer to emotional hurts.* Usually when we think of Christ's work on the cross, we emphasize that He died in our stead that we might be freed from sin. What is less known is that the same death took place that we might have emotional freedom. In Isaiah 53:4, we learn that Christ identified Himself with our feelings: "Surely our griefs He Him-self bore, and our sorrows He carried." Isaiah predicted that the Spirit of the Lord would come upon Christ and anoint Him "to bring good news to the afflicted; He has sent me to bind up the brokenhearted, to proclaim liber-ty to captives, and freedom to prisoners" (Isa. 61:1). Just as the cross represents an exchange for our sin—our sin is imputed to Christ and His righteousness is imputed to us—so it is with our emotional responses. As we commit ourselves to Him, He brings about emotional wholeness so that we might be able to live out His life in us.

I'm not implying that we should expect to live in per-petual emotional tranquillity, for Christ Himself experi-enced grief, sorrow, rejection, and depression. But He was able to endure them because of the triumph of His obedience. Paul explained that redemption was accom-plished for the body, soul, and spirit. And although total deliverance will only take place when we are in heaven, we can begin to benefit from that redemption *now*. The cross includes deliverance from emotional slavery.

Think of it this way: suppose you lived in an apartment complex in which the landlord harassed you, charging exorbitant rent and blackmailing you. You became filled with fear, anxiety, guilt, and depression. Yet there was nothing you could do, for you were captive to this intruder. But let us suppose that a new landlord buys the apartment complex. He is kind and considerate, and rather than using intimidation, he lavishes you with love. Now what if your former landlord returned and began to demand your allegiance once again? Of course you wouldn't pay him. You'd tell him to take up the matter with the new landlord and then firmly shut the door! That's what Christ has given us the authority to do, because we as believers are under new management. The taxing emotional burdens of the past need no longer be carried by us, for we have a new owner. And when He said, "You shall know the truth, and the truth shall make you free" (John 8:32), that freedom included release from emotional slavery. Because of the cross, no feelings need rule over us.

3. *The Body of Christ must provide a strong emotional acceptance.* Yes, God accepts us, but He also wants His people to demonstrate acceptance one to another. Many people today grow up without a sense of identity. Those who are adopted often daydream endlessly about who their real parents were or why they were given away. Others may experience severe feelings of rejection for innumerable reasons. They grow up without a sense of "belongingness." They may have no family roots, no sense of social acceptance. The church must realize that emotional healing takes place best within the context of caring Christians who not only bear their

own burdens but share those of others. I've met people delivered from depression when five or six fellow Christians have decided that they would intercede until the emotional release came. With small support groups, those who have never felt the warmth of human affection and acceptance will begin to have a sense of identity.

Yet, there are thousands today who will not take the risk of friendship. They've been hurt so many times that they have become loners, hardened to the hurts that are destroying them. Here again, we all must reach out so that others will see that we do care, that friendships can be built and trust repaired. Every one of us needs someone who will love us regardless of what we do. And if we have no such friends, we must seek them within the confines of the Christian church.

A word of caution is in order. Often, those who have experienced rejection will find other Christians and plague them with endless promises and smother them with a desire for emotional support. As a result, such people usually encounter more rejection because they unwittingly give the impression that they are an emotional drain to anyone who begins to befriend them. Here again we must be sensitive to people's needs, but at the same time, we cannot let others use guilt as a motivation for our own behavior. We can support those in emotional turbulence, but there does come a time when they must also stand alone, fully responsible for their own behavior and reactions to life. Small caring communities within the church are necessary, however, for people to grow in emotional maturity.

4. *We must have a wholesome self-image.* This can only come about when we cease believing what our emotions tell us and begin to believe what God says about us. We are confronted by two pictures of ourselves.

One is of us as we are in Christ: Sons of God; indwelt by the Holy Spirit; joined to the Son; considered as God's special possession; and assured of future glorification. Then there is another picture of what some of us are like in the world, the world of our emotions: pessimistic, guilt-ridden, irritable, touchy, depressed, and worthless. Faced with such an apparent contradiction, we must make a choice. Shall we believe what God has said, or shall we follow the path of least resistance and give in to our feelings? It boils down to this: Which portrait shall we live by?

Clearly, we face a dilemma. Our emotions, inclinations, and circumstances point in one direction, whereas God's description of us points in another. We cannot live by both, for they cancel each other. Faith means that we must not merely believe what God has said, but we must also *disbelieve* what our experiences seem to tell us.

Can our inclinations and observations actually be wrong? If I see myself as unloved, unacceptable to God, and powerless, might I be mistaken? Yes!

Left to our private observations, we would conclude that the sun revolves around the earth. What could be more obvious than that the earth is stationary and the sun moves from east to west? Yet that conclusion is dead wrong. Astronomers tell us that the sun never rises; rather, the earth turns, tilting on its axis toward the sun. Our common-sense conclusions can be misleading.

So it is with our interpretation of the events of life. Hunches and feelings are not a reliable guide to understanding the real you; God's statements invalidate our distorted self-image. If He says He loves us—and He does so repeatedly—then we *are* loved whether we feel like it or not. If we have been seated in heavenly places, we *are* in God's presence even when He seems distant. In Christ, our acceptance before God is complete and secure even when we are disappointed in ourselves.

Victory, then, is not "feeling just right." It is found by faith and faith alone. And whenever faith runs counter to feeling, we must accept faith in God's Word as the true barometer of circumstances. A few years ago, an airplane crashed into the top of a mountain. The reason? Prior to the crash, the pilot realized that his instrument panel had gone askew. The plane's equipment indicated he was flying off course and headed for disaster. But the pilot knew better. His intuitive sense of direction told him that the instruments were wrong and his own judgment of the terrain beneath was reliable. Within an hour he crashed.

The irony was that his judgment was *not* correct. The mechanical instruments were accurate. If he had followed their readings and rejected his own intuition, the crash would not have occurred. God wants us to fly with His equipment, the Word of God. Concentrating on who He says we are helps close the gap between our experience and our theology.

5. *We must see joy as a by-product of obedience.* Many people seek happiness and never find it because it is never found when you seek it directly. Happiness is part of the blessing that comes from doing the will of God.

Perhaps a better word than happiness is *joy.* John the Baptist said that his joy was complete. He was a voice crying in the wilderness. As such, he did not draw attention to himself or speak of his gifts, but he humbly stated his calling as a servant of the Lord.

In ancient times, the friend of the bridegroom was responsible to bring the bride to the bridegroom, and after introducing them in the marriage ceremony, the friend stepped quietly away. In John 3:29, John the Baptist used this custom as an illustration of his relationship to Jesus Christ. His responsibiluty was to introduce people to the Bridegroom and then fade into the background. It was this that completed John's joy.

His satisfaction did not come from the large crowds that gathered to hear him preach near the Jordan. He was not jealous of Christ's popularity, and when people left him to follow his Master, he was not grieved. Today there is much advice on how to find lasting happiness. Most of these suggestions stress the need to have well-defined goals such as self-fulfillment, a challenging career, or making money. At root, these recommendations are sinful. John the Baptist summarized what our goal should be when he said regarding Christ, "He must increase, but I must decrease" (John 3:30). John's whole life was lived to the glory of Christ.

Let's remember that the joy of the Holy Spirit does not come by seeking self-fulfillment; it comes by seeking Christ's fulfillment.

Joy (emotional stability, if you will) is a fruit of the Holy Spirit. It comes when we accept death to our own plans and ambitions and receive what Christ has for us. Without ending our self-rule and putting Christ completely in charge, there is no route to emotional wholeness. Someone has rightly said, "Joy is the flag flown from the castle of the heart when the King is in residence there."

If anyone should use the emotional trauma of his past as an excuse for continuing as an emotional cripple, let him ponder the nine qualities that are listed in Galatians 5:22-23 as the fruit of the Spirit. Notice that either directly or indirectly, each one touches our emotional lives: love, joy, peace, patience, kindness, goodness, faithfulness, gentleness, self-control. What a picture of emotional stability!

These are the qualities that the Holy Spirit wants to form in us as we obey God's Word. Obedience precedes blessing. Christ endured the holocaust of Gethsemane by knowing that in the end He would have emotional satisfaction (Heb. 12:2). He obeyed although He didn't feel like it; the feelings came later. No, we can't expect a life without emotional turbulence, but there can be emotional healing; the Spirit can work even amid our ups and downs. God wants us to manage our emotions; He's assured us that they need not manage us.

The following pages introduce us to what the Bible has to say about some of the more common emotions. We've tried to stress how to manage those emotions, how to let God achieve emotional stability in our lives. If these chapters should help someone along the path to emotional wholeness, the purpose of this book will have been accomplished.

Suggested Application

1. What is the basis for emotional wholeness according to the apostle Paul in Ephesians 1:3-7 and 2:4-10?

2. What is the basis for emotional disturbance according to Galatians 5:19-21?

3. What is the responsibility of believers in relation to a person who is deeply troubled (Acts 20:35; Rom. 15:1; Gal. 6:2; Heb. 13:3)?

4. Select a passage of Scripture to memorize as a guard against the attempts of Satan to lead you into emotional distress. Consider Psalm 23; Romans 8:35-39; 2 Corinthians 2:14; 1 John 3:1-2; 4:9-11; 5:4.

3

Those Feelings of Love

HIS WIFE'S words cut worse than any whip could.

"I don't love you. I have *never* loved you."

She sat on the edge of the bed with her back to him, head down. She paused, waiting for the courage to continue.

"I married you because I was overawed by you, and because I wanted to get away from home. I've been absolutely miserable. Cathy finally persuaded me to tell you. She said you'd understand."

He wanted to take her in his arms, for there was no doubt in his mind that he had always loved her. But he feared rejection. As his wife's confession continued, Jim stood up, walked to the window, and stared outside. He could scarcely believe what he was hearing. He had thought he knew his wife well, but now she was revealing a part of her feelings he had never known before. *Just imagine,* he thought to himself, *I've lived seven years of my life with a woman who doesn't love me.* He felt betrayed, cheated. Either Sue entered the relationship unsure about those elusive feelings of love, or something happened that doused the flame.

Is there a way to manage those feelings of love so that a lasting relationship can be established? It all begins with falling in love, doesn't it? Let's consider a sequence of events that has happened a thousand times: John carefully selects a college that will give him the major he needs to achieve his vocational goals. Not many days into the first quarter, he is attracted to Mary, who sits a couple of rows over in one of his classes. Much to his delight, John discovers that she finds him attractive as well. In a few weeks they are sure they are in love. But near the end of the quarter, there's a perceptible change. John begins to wonder what he saw in Mary, and she begins to wonder what she saw in John.

The next semester, John is dating Martha. This relationship lasts a little longer before Martha decides it won't work. John is a little slow getting the message, but he is eventually convinced. One year after he graduates, he marries Jan.

Now suppose John and Mary had rushed off during the quarter break and married. Three months later they would have begun to wonder what they saw in each other. That initial romantic aura would be gone and the reality of living together would be setting in. Then let us suppose that Jan appears on the scene. It doesn't take long for John to realize that she has a lot more to offer than Sue, that his heart is doing things it never has done with Sue. Now what?

Little wonder that someone has suggested that getting married is a bit like eating mushrooms—you are not exactly sure if it's the thing you ought to do until it is too late! You discover that in marriage there is a certain amount of risk, for there is always the possibility that if you had waited, someone better might have come along. In fact, in our mobile society, she or he may very well appear after the third company move.

Then there's the kind of situation you may get into in Christian work, or even on the job. You have time on your hands, so you volunteer for secretarial work at church. You thought you were happily married, but one day you wake up and say to yourself, "I've fallen in love with the pastor." Your emotions are in absolute turmoil; you know that's not the way it's supposed to be, but what do you do about those feelings?

We can only begin to understand these kinds of feelings, these emotional responses to other people, if we realize the clear biblical distinction between human love (affection) and divine love. In Matthew 5:46 and 47, Jesus established what normal human love is like: "For if you love those who love you, what reward have you? Do not even the tax-gatherers do the same? And if you greet your brothers only, what do you do more than others? Do not even the Gentiles do the same?" Jesus reminded His listeners that *human love depends on the one loved.* You salute the person in the marketplace who salutes you. You are kind to your brothers because they are kind to you. You perhaps like someone and are attracted to him because he does something for you. Your response is conditioned by what the other person does.

Two things normally attract us to someone we meet, his personality or her looks (or vice versa). Some time ago I met a West-Coast pastor whom I had never seen before. Yet within fifteen minutes we were chatting like old friends. We could talk about anything, it seemed, because there was a genuine sense of harmony. That's a human reaction when you meet someone with a personality that makes you feel good and to which you respond easily.

Whether we like to admit it or not, all of us tend to respond to others on the basis of their appearance. Statistics prove that the cute child, the physically attractive teen, gets the breaks in life. If there is a dispute in school and two children are fighting, the teacher will normally discipline the one who is not as good-looking as the other. Hollywood has strengthened that basic human reaction so that we unconsciously accept people on the basis of their appearance. Add the powerful stimulus of sexual attractiveness and you've got a strong force with which to contend. And if the person has an attractive personality as well, there is a tremendously powerful package. No wonder people "fall in love" with such a person.

The Bible is aware of such human love, beautifully described in a poem by Solomon: "How beautiful you are, my darling, how beautiful you are! Your eyes are like doves behind your veil; your hair is like a flock of goats that have descended from Mount Gilead. . . . Your lips are like a scarlet thread, and your mouth is lovely. Your temples are like a slice of pomegranate behind your veil" (Song of Sol. 4:1, 3). Is it any wonder that people say love is blind? Mind you, the neighbors are not, but love is!

Now notice what else he says: "You are altogether beautiful, my darling, and there is no blemish in you. . . . You have made my heart beat faster, my sister, my bride; you have made my heart beat faster with a single glance of your eyes, with a single strand of your necklace. How beautiful is your love, my sister, my bride! How much better is your love than wine, and the fragrance of your oils than all kinds of spices!" (Song of Sol. 4:7, 9-10). That man was in love!

Is there anything wrong with that kind of human love? No, of course not. Human love is God-ordained and God-given; it makes life exciting. Not only does it add spice to life, but it is absolutely essential if we are to be emotionally well-balanced. Yet it has clear limitations.

In the first place, *human love is subject to change.* Why?

Because it depends on the one being loved, it needs to be fed by the stimulus that the one loved provides. If that changes, love may change.

A lady came up to me after I spoke at a large church in the Midwest. I thought she was physically attractive, but she had a cast on her arm and part of her face was scarred. With her was her four-year-old daughter. She told me about a fire at their house two years earlier in which she had been severely burned. She was placed in the hospital and underwent extensive treatment because of the severity of the burns. Even after two years, she was still in a partial body cast. When her husband saw how extensive the scars were and that they would never disappear, he left her. He "fell in love" with a younger girl and married her, leaving his former wife with the care of the four-year-old.

Remember the old adage "Love conquers all"? Don't you believe it! Human love has clear limits because it is based on something in you or about you—it's to my advantage to be associated with you. No wonder one or the other spouse asks for a divorce because "You are not fun to live with anymore" or "You are no longer the beautiful person I married."

There is a second limitation to that human feeling called love, and that is its *transferability*. That is the best word I can think of to describe what I have in mind. You see, as long as we love one person on a human level, it is easy on a human level to learn to love others, to "fall in love" with others. This is particularly true of the marriage relationship.

Remember John? It is quite possible for him to marry that girl he met his first semester—yes, he believes he is in love with Mary. But when he meets Jan, he can quickly transfer his feelings to her because she represents more of his ideal in a woman. Human love is always transferable because it depends on what the other person can do for me.

Ever think of how little guidance the Bible gives about the right person to marry? Certainly that is not because it is an unimportant decision. I believe that the reason the Bible's only advice is to marry a believer is that God does not want us to become paranoid wondering whether we married the right partner, whether exactly *that* person will always fulfill us, will always be beautiful, will always say just the right thing. God wants us to realize that marriage cannot be based on human attractiveness alone. There is far more in the Bible on learning how to love than on how to discern whether you have fallen in love with the right person.

My wife is a very attractive person. She is easy to love on a human level. I consider myself fortunate and thank God for her. Yet even in our marriage, we have discovered that there are times when human love is not enough. That's why the Bible tells us about divine love—so that we can go on loving at such times, for very few marriages can make it on human love alone (and the divorce statistics bear that out).

When you get to divine love, you are in another ballgame altogether. *Divine love is based on and dependent on the lover.* It is not a feeling, for with it we can even love our enemies. Clearly, if that love were a feeling, God would be putting a burden on us that we could not bear. He would be asking us to do the impossible, for there is no way we can have a nice, comfortable feeling about an enemy.

The first characteristic that makes divine love radically different from human love is that divine love always involves *sacrificial action.* The Bible says in Romans 5:8, "But God demonstrates His own love toward us, in that while we were yet sinners, Christ died for us." Long before we could respond to God, He was already responding to us.

Sometimes I meet people who say, "Oh, I just love the world. I just love the whole world." No, they don't! You cannot love people you have never met. You cannot divinely love someone unless you have sacrificed on his behalf. Often, what people mean when they say they love the world is that there is pity in their heart for people in other countries. There may be a sense in which they may feel sentimentally involved with the needs of the world. Divine love, however, is more than sentiment. It always refers to sacrificial action. That is why you will see people who say they love the world but who are unable to get along with a neighbor, a son-in-law, or an aged parent. They have not sacrificed—nor are they about to—for those people.

Remember Jesus' command to "Love your enemies"? If that kind of love is divine and involves sacrificial action, Jesus should indicate the kind of action expected, should He not? And He does. The first action Jesus commands is, "Bless those who curse you" (Luke 6:28). Negatively, that means that you do not speak evil of them, that there is no indiscriminate discussion of experiences. This actually only ingrains the hurt. Positively, it means that you actually learn to say good things about your enemy.

Sometimes in marriage counseling, I have asked the husband to write down five good things about his wife, and vice versa. They usually discover that there are more than five commendable qualities about their spouses, even though they chew on their pens for a while before getting started. Once we begin to find good things to say, we should have them at the ready when our "enemy's" name comes up in conversation so we can bless him instead of cursing him.

We need to go beyond even that. We need to actually wish them well. We must believe that God loves them just as much as He loves us. When Jesus said "Bless those who curse you," He was asking us to say those things that will be a credit to them instead of an attempt to exploit their weaknesses. Have you considered how this would affect your relationship with your ex-husband or ex-wife if you are separated or divorced?

Jesus provided another action suggestion: "Do good to those who hate you" (Luke 6:27). In another setting, the Bible reminds us to feed an enemy if he is hungry and give him a drink if he is thirsty (Rom. 12:20). Scripturally, we take positive action whether we feel like it or not. The reason was spelled out by Jesus in Matthew 5:45: "For He causes His sun to rise on the evil and the good, and sends rain on the righteous and the unrighteous." God blesses without discrimination, and so should we.

The third command by Jesus is, "Pray for those who mistreat you" (Luke 6:28). Jesus Christ on the cross gave us a beautiful example of this when He prayed, "Father, forgive them; for they do not know what they are doing" (Luke 23:34). Remember Stephen, after the stones had started striking him, praying, "Lord, do not hold this sin against them!" (Acts 7:60).

We ought to pray that those who have wronged us will be forgiven by God. We ought to pray earnestly that they will experience the richness of the Father's love and forgiveness. Then we also ought to pray that God will bless them and make their life a blessing. That's divine love in action.

There's a fourth command I would like to add on the basis of other passages in the New Testament, and that is that we ought to depend on the Holy Spirit. There is a supernatural giving that the Holy Spirit is able to work within us. We discover that we cannot love in a given situation, but when we learn to depend on the Holy Spirit, He gives us the motivation to actually take the initiative. When we finally begin to initiate action, we discover that we really do begin to love again, to love our enemies.

That is how you really gain control over your feelings. When you begin to obey the Word of God, He takes those actions of love and begins to rebuild the human affections drained away through the pressures of life. So even though human love may have disappeared, God can rebuild those feelings of affection as we start acting as Jesus commanded.

You say, "You do not really know what you are talking about. You have never been abused the way I have been abused." Maybe I haven't, but I am only too well aware of how people treat each other. I can readily understand why in many relationships there are no feelings left, why the very things that were once attractive to you now cause you to feel revulsion toward that person. Human love simply is not strong enough to weather all the storms of life. But when we begin to exercise divine love, which is not a feeling based on sentiment or upon whether you fulfill me or not, but an action taken as a result of my commitment to you, then God can mend the relationship. You will experience the tremendous power of God's love as you actually do what Jesus commanded.

A woman who had been sexually abused by her stepfather from the age of seventeen on into her early twenties married a fine man. She discovered that she could not love her husband, because as soon as he showed her any affection, it would elicit all those ugly feelings of hatred she had toward her stepfather. She came to her pastor for counseling as a last resort.

"Your first step is to forgive your stepfather. If you do not forgive him, there is no hope of your ever loving your husband," the pastor told her very kindly. He knew she represented many people who cannot really love because they have never forgiven someone who abused them. He asked her to turn to the passage of Scripture that gives us the action plan for loving our enemies, and he worked out a homework assignment. She was so desperate that she decided to go ahead with the assignment.

I guess she did a little archaeological work, because she did come up with some good things to say about her stepfather. She discovered, much to her surprise, that he had some good qualities. She actually practiced saying some of those good things. Whenever a conversation would start about her past life or regarding him, she would be sure to say something good. She refused to make any insinuations or negative remarks. You will remember that God says He judges us by the words that come out of our mouths, for if we speak evil it only increases the evil. If we speak good, God is responsible for multiplying the good.

She also remembered that her stepfather had a birthday coming up. So she baked a cake for his birthday. And because the Bible says to pray for your enemy, she determined to pray for him three times a day. She said, "I am going to pray that God will forgive his sin and that he will be brought to repentance. I am going to pray that God will bless him. I am going to pray that God is going to use that man and change him for God's glory." And she did it.

How did she feel about doing all this? In reality, every fiber of her body revolted against the idea. She would have been a hypocrite if she had said at that time, "I really love this man." But obedience to God's Word is never hypocrisy. So despite how she felt, she went about her assignment week in and week out. Several weeks later, she saw her stepfather in a supermarket. She noticed he was buying some groceries and then watched him walk to his car. Suddenly she noticed that her feelings had changed. Instead of all those ugly feelings of hurt and bitterness that always surfaced when she saw him, she realized that she actually had some human affection for him. Feelings of human love arose toward him. She later told her pastor, "If it were not for our past relationship, I would have gone and put my arm around him." Then she added, "Furthermore, I now love my husband." She had experienced that human feelings can be managed when they are overwhelmed by divine love.

Some time ago I had the privilege of visiting a church on the West Coast that had been in a state of perpetual revival. The church had tripled in attendance in six years. I asked the pastor what the secret of this growth was. He said, "The great thing that changed this church happened when we taught them to love one another rather than simply disagreeing all the time. We were having all kinds of bitter strife because of the natural differences of opinion that exist whenever you put people together."

Human love is a response to good things happening to us. Divine love is triggered by an act of the will. That's why an act of commitment to love as God has loved us gets our feelings under divine management.

Can Sue actually learn to love Jim? The answer is yes. She must choose to say no to herself—her cherished dreams, her fantasies. She can no longer think of whom she ought to have married and what that other man could have done for her. No longer can she daydream about how someone else would have made her *feel*.

Such feelings of self-pity must be confessed for what they are: sin. Then she must begin a positive course of action, in dependence upon the Holy Spirit. She must meditate in the Scriptures (memorizing 1 Corinthians 13 would be a good beginning), because at root, her problem is spiritual. Since she needs divine love, *her relationship with her husband will be determined by her relationship with God.* God will use this experience in her life to strengthen her relationship with Him. Remember, divine love involves a choice, dependence, and faith. We can learn to love *anyone.*

Suggested Application

1. The best exposition of divine love is 1 Corinthians 13. Here Paul listed fifteen qualities of love. Write down each one with a practical example to illustrate it.

2. "The reason people can't get along is sin—take sin away and the bickering is over." Do you agree or disagree? Give examples of the kinds of sin that create conflict within the home. What kind of conflict may not be the result of sin?

3. Meditate on 1 John 4:18-19. Why can fear and love not coexist?

4. Love being a gift of the Holy Spirit, how does Paul teach that we can receive the Spirit's power (Gal. 5:18-26)?

5. What should a married person do who is falling in love with another partner? Specifically, what steps should be taken to prevent physical and emotional

involvement? Answers can be found to keep oneself from sexual sin by reading Proverbs 5.

Defeating Depression

BEAUTIFUL. Intelligent. Well-adjusted. Those adjectives describe the woman who came to see me after a meeting. She told me that although she was quite wealthy and even had a reasonably happy marriage, she was contemplating suicide. She along with millions of others was suffering from America's number one emotional disorder: depression.

Perhaps depression is the darkest of all negative emotions. It's been described in various ways. Someone has called it "a dark tunnel with not a ray of light." Another refers to it as the time when "your emotions weigh a ton and you want to die."

No one seems to be immune. A pastor admitted he was so depressed that when he crossed a street, he wished a car would hit him so that he would be free from his emotional misery. A highly respected religious leader says that he experiences times of depression so severe that he finds it difficult to get out of bed in the morning.

Experts vary in their analysis of what causes such emotional blackouts. In some instances the cause could be physical; exhaustion and fatigue can trigger depression. Or it can be caused by disappointments in life. Recently, I spoke to someone who had lost his job, whose marriage was falling apart, and who consequently suffered depression. Such cases, of course, are usually not too severe, because when circumstances improve, the emotional trauma begins to subside.

Sometimes depression is related to future concerns that weigh heavily upon our minds. Even Jesus Christ, who was sinless, experienced a form of depression in Gethsemane when He was contemplating the horror of becoming identified with the sins of the whole world. Often depression comes about because of immediate circumstances, and release comes when these situations are rectified. Short periods of depression are common to us all.

However, there are those who live with depression despite favorable circumstances and a life relatively free of tragedy. I've known those who have experienced depression for twenty or thirty years, often going from one counselor to another, seeking release from their emotional heaviness. Often they are encouraged to take drugs to alleviate the emotional pain they experience. As a result, they never do uncover the root of the problem; the symptoms may disappear, but the cause is still there.

Many counselors agree that the three chief causes of depression are guilt, rejection, and the related emotion of self-pity. I am aware that not all cases of depression can be reduced to one of these three causes. Depression may be stimulated by physically or medically related conditions. For some it comes without warning and for no apparent reason. We ought not to assume that all who struggle with this emotional burden are out of fellowship with God.

Yet I believe that in the majority of instances, depression is caused by tensions that can be eased through spiritual counsel. Depression usually is a sign that our spiritual antenna is plugged into the wrong channel; we are out of tune with God.

Since rejection is so common, we'll consider those feelings in more detail in a later chapter. For now, let's concentrate on guilt and self-pity.

Let's talk first about guilt. Many people still underestimate the effect of guilt in a person's life. For example, I've heard people who are living in sexual immorality say, "We've learned to work through our guilt." What they really mean is that they have learned to ignore the guilt or to talk themselves out of it. We forget that the consequences of sin are built into the nature of man and the world. We cannot violate God's commandments without choking our relationship with Him. Disobedience *always* has its consequences.

Can guilt cause a depression severe enough to lead to suicide? Consider Judas, the man who betrayed Christ. When he saw that Jesus Christ had been condemned, he felt remorse and returned the thirty pieces of silver to the chief priests. Of course they were not sympathetic to his half-hearted confession, "I have sinned by betraying innocent blood." So he threw the silver into the sanctuary and departed, then went and hanged himself (Matt. 27:3-5).

What led to the guilt-ridden remorse that Judas experienced? In a word it was greed, his insatiable desire for money. He was the treasurer of the disciples and apparently had been pilfering all along. Yet, he did not receive enough money to satisfy himself. He needed more.

The example of Judas reminds us that sin never satisfies. You can never say, "I've had enough." A woman involved in an illicit relationship told me, "I'm going to see that man just one more time." Do you think that was the end of it? Of course not. No one trapped in a sinful habit is satisfied; rather, the impulses to do evil only become stronger.

Judas loved money, silver in particular. He thought that with thirty extra pieces he would get ahead financially. Before he betrayed Christ, his focus was on the money; doubtless he visualized all that he would be able to purchase with it. But after he had the money in his hands, he began to think of his sin; the money meant nothing. The satisfaction of having silver was overshadowed by the weight of guilt that he experienced. No doubt if Judas had lived in our time, he could have talked to his psychiatrist and received some drugs to deaden the pain of his deep remorse. But since such help was not open to him, he did what seventy thousand Americans do every year. He committed suicide.

It's important to notice that Judas's remorse was exploited by Satan. You'll recall that after the Lord had assembled the disciples for the Last Supper, Satan personally entered into Judas to enable him to betray Christ. We have no reason to think that Judas asked for Satan's help. It's just that this man had given territory in his life to satanic impulses, and Satan assumed he had a right to Judas's life. Remember that Satan and his demons need no formal welcome. All that he seeks is an unbeliever hostile to the truth or a Christian who lives in persistent sin, and he will take as much territory as he can get.

Further evidence that evil spirits can inflame the emotion of depression comes from the life of Saul. You'll recall that "an evil spirit from the LORD terrorized him" (1 Sam. 16:14). God allowed a demon to torment him, and as a result he experienced times of deep melancholy and depression. This explains why David was able to help Saul overcome his emotional problems. When

David played his harp, the king felt better. Evil spirits cannot easily tolerate music that exhalts the power of the Lord. When David came to play praises to the Lord, the spirit withdrew and Saul returned to normalcy.

What did Judas and Saul have in common? Both were disobedient to God; both gave territory in their lives to evil; and both experienced depression. For Judas it was covetousness, for Saul it was pride, for others it is sexual sin. No matter. The result is the same: morbid guilt, melancholy, depression.

Of course, guilt can cause depression even when we may not be able to pinpoint any specific sin in our lives. I know a woman who was constantly told by her father, "God is going to punish you for your disobedience." And since every child has moments of disobedience, this woman in later life interpreted every tragedy as a fulfillment of her father's words. One day when she and her husband were on vacation, had two flat tires, and couldn't find a place to spend the night, she became so depressed that she wanted to jump out of the car and run away. Fortunately, she has since learned the cure for such depression.

Today there are many people who are under the condemnation of God, or at least believe they are, who experience uninterrupted depression. With the rise of abortions, divorces, and other sinful behavior patterns, we should not be surprised that depression is rampant in our society. Guilt feelings inflamed by evil spirits who accuse believers before the throne of God day and night provide the combination that fuels the dull flames of emotional heaviness.

The second major cause for depression is self-pity. Recently, I received a phone call from a girl who wanted help to escape from the cycle of suicidal depression. A few of my questions immediately brought deep resentment to the surface. She was angry with her father, who had left the family to live with a teenage girl. She was bitter against her friends at church, who she felt had not accepted her. She was resentful of her mother and brother; her bitterness was deep and vindictive.

Expressions of self-pity almost always surface among those who are depressed. Many hours are spent rehearsing in great detail all the wrongs done against them. Often the depressed person prays but receives no relief, because even the prayer time is used to recount all the wrongs done against him or her. Every insult, whether real or imagined, is meticulously added to the list of reasons why they have a "right" to be bitter.

Let me stress that we must be sensitive to such people. With the breakup of families and the alarming rise of child abuse, many people have indeed been treated unfairly. Our world is filled with injustice. We can readily understand why resentment and self-pity develop. But although we must show compassion, we cannot sympathize with those in such an emotional quandary lest they begin to think that we agree that they have a right to feel the way they do. For unless they give up that right, the depression will never leave.

I have found that many people deeply resent being told they are wallowing in self-pity. Even when it becomes clear that such is the case, they resist the idea that they must give up their right to feel sorry for themselves. Sometimes they walk out of the office and slam the door or hang up the telephone. Yet by insisting on their right to continue in their present thought patterns, they are closing the door to freedom.

How can we help those who are filled with guilt, self-pity, or the feeling of inferiority that so often accompanies these destructive emotions? Some counselors would tell us that such a person must become strong so that he will learn to cope; he must adjust to the storms of life without being victimized by these emotional hurts. But in becoming strong, the person often becomes bitter, determined never to let any person affect his emotional equilibrium again. Often he withdraws, determined never to risk another friendship lest he be rejected and the hurt become greater.

However, the teaching of the Bible is not that we must become strong, but rather that we must become weak. Only those who understand that they cannot cope, that they are unable to solve their own emotional problems, are able to find deliverance.

Let's use David's prayer in Psalm 51 as an example of someone who overcame his guilt and depression after being guilty of adultery and murder. Remember that David had committed those two sins with deliberate forethought. Even if we should say that his adultery was the result of immediate passion, the murder of Uriah was planned over a period of several days. Not only was there no sacrifice available for those sins, but no restitution could be made for what had happened. David's tears could never restore the purity of Bathsheba, nor would his regret ever bring a dead man back to life. What had been done had been done, and the consequences could not be reversed. Furthermore, David's sin was of the most troubling kind because it directly affected the lives of those within his own family. He forfeited his ability to effectively discipline his children because he himself had fallen into serious sin. The child of Bathsheba died as a further judgment of God. Yet, despite all these factors, David was restored to fellowship with God, and his heavy depression vanished.

Here are some of the steps that we need to follow when overcome by the depression-guilt syndrome.

First, *we must admit that of ourselves we have no answer to our emotional turbulence.* David cast himself wholly upon the lovingkindness and mercy of God (Psalm 51:1). If we try to repress our emotions by saying, "I'll make it on my own, I won't have anything to do with those who have hurt me," we are only becoming hardened in our bitterness. Only those who give up will be taken in by God. Actually, the root of all guilt and self-pity is self-rule, the innate desire we have to be our own king, to be the master of our own destiny. When Lucifer sinned, a drop of the poison of his rebellion fell on every human heart. And just as Satan himself is filled with hostility toward God, so we, left to ourselves, want to be our own king. We want to keep our rights to bitterness and make our own choices. We think that if we want to have illicit relationships, that's up to us; we're not interested in having God direct our lives. The result is the emotions we've mentioned: guilt, self-pity, resentment.

Such feelings should not be ignored. They are a painful witness to the fact that something is wrong, that spiritually we've gone astray. To suppress them is to shun the warning signals that have been established by God to let us know we are out of harmony with His divine plan. Physical pain is a reminder that we must see a doctor; emotional pain is God shouting at us, asking whether we've finally decided to meet Him on His terms.

When David was pointedly confronted with his sin, he ended his rationalizations and faced himself honestly. He knew then that he had no reason for God to accept him apart from God's mercy. He also knew that he had no resources to commend himself to God.

Centuries after the time of David, Jesus Christ died on the cross to provide a complete work that would be the basis for our emotional wholeness. From the cross we receive many benefits, two of which are forgiveness for our sins and deliverance from self-rule. All who believe in Christ become immediately identified with Him in His death, burial, resurrection, and ascension. We must grasp this truth by faith before it will be applied to our experience. Self-rule (the Bible often refers to it as "the flesh") is so strong that it cannot be broken by ourselves; we must trust Christ to do it. And the Bible teaches that He has already done it for those who are willing to accept it (Rom. 6-8).

What is the first step in coping with guilt and self-pity? It is to once and for all admit our complete helplessness and bring our lives to God, accepting His mercy and claiming His power to do what we cannot. Our struggle against God must end. We can no longer fight our emotions; instead, we must become dependent on divine help *alone.*

Second, *like David, we must take full responsibility for our sin* (vv. 2-4). No doubt he had spent many hours rationalizing his behavior. After all, God had made Bathsheba so beautiful; furthermore, she happened to be taking a bath at exactly the time when he was resting on the roof of his house. Also, kings in those days were allowed to have many wives, so what David did was consistent with the behavior of the monarchs at that point in history. He reminds me of a man who lived in adultery and rationalized, *I have emotional needs that must be met. After all, I'm a human being even though I am a Christian.* But in the presence of God, all excuses fall by the wayside. We must see ourselves as fully responsible for all our actions, even those that have been brought about by someone else's misbehavior. David saw himself alone in the presence of God, defenseless and without a single objection to whatever God would want to do.

He also realized that his sin was primarily against God. Listen to his words: "Against Thee, Thee only, I have sinned, and done what is evil in Thy sight, so that Thou art justified when Thou dost speak, and blameless when Thou dost judge" (v. 4). His guilt could not be "worked through" in therapy or by the taking of tranquilizers. Even if no one had found out about his sin, even if there would have been no visible consequences, he would have had to face God on the matter that weighed heavily on his mind. Too often we think that we can control the consequences of our disobedience, not realizing that our primary obligation is to God, not our husband, wife, or children. A woman may have an abortion secretly and thus assume that she will not encounter any emotional consequences. But her relationship with friends is not really as important as her relationship with God. Yes, her parents may be hurt and offended, but God more so. David finally realized that his sin against Uriah and Bathsheba was ultimately a sin against God.

Third, *David knew, as we must, that he needed cleansing as well as forgiveness for his sin.* Yes, there is a difference. Forgiveness has to do with our legal standing in the sight of God; when He forgives us, we are credited with Christ's righteousness and accepted before God. But it is possible for someone to be forgiven and not feel forgiven. David prayed, "Wash me thoroughly from my iniquity, and cleanse me from my sin" (v. 2). Cleansing is the subjective application of forgiveness. Let me put it this way: forgiveness is what God does *outside* us. It is His statement that He no longer holds our sins against us. Cleansing is what God does *inside* us, purifying our minds from sin. This is confirmed in 1 John 1:9, where both aspects of God's work are given: "If we confess our sins, He is faithful and righteous to forgive us our sins and to cleanse us from all unrighteousness."

Perhaps you have come to Christ to accept His forgiveness, but you still feel guilty. Remember that your feelings will only catch up to your theology when you insist on cleansing so that your mind and conscience are clean rather than controlled by those nagging feelings of guilt. Once you have confessed a specific sin, you need not confess it again. You simply have to accept the cleansing that is yours by faith.

David understood that there was a direct relationship between his cleansing and emotional peace of heart. He said, "Make me to hear joy and gladness, let the bones which Thou hast broken rejoice" (v. 8). In Psalm 32, David spoke of the anxiety and depression he felt before he confessed his sin. He wrote, "When I kept silent about my sin, my body wasted away through my groaning all day long. For day and night Thy hand was heavy upon me; my vitality was drained away as with the fever heat of summer" (vv. 3-4). Guilt had created an emotional logjam; forgiveness let the rivers of joy flow again. David learned that a glad heart does not come by suppressing sin but by confessing and forsaking it.

Guilt is not simply a feeling that we have to unlearn. It is not the result of a repressive society but is our God-given response to moral failure. No amount of escape through drugs, sex, or diversionary pleasure can erase a nagging conscience. But forgiveness and cleansing are available for all men through Christ.

Almost every satanic attack is directed toward our conscience. Evil spirits desire to make us feel foul, dirty, and beyond hope. Such feelings cannot be met by trying to convince ourselves that we are otherwise. There is, after all, no good thing within us; we have no inner resources to meet such an attack. Our only hope is to find an objective basis for forgiveness. Christ's sacrifice on the cross meets that requirement. So let me say it again: *You can be both forgiven and cleansed by admitting your sin to God and accepting Christ's death for you.* That can be done now, whether you feel like it or not.

Finally, David began to praise God once again. He prayed, "O LORD, open my lips, that my mouth may declare Thy praise" (Psalm 51:15). One of the best antidotes for depression is praise. Anyone who is able to choose to thank God for the circumstances of life suddenly experiences the release of God's power. Praise means that we believe that God is able to work in spite of our difficulties, that He uses the heartaches and emotional struggles of life to teach us lessons about Himself that we could learn in no other way.

Earlier in this chapter we noted that self-pity is a predominant cause of depression. Self-pity is sin because it denies the Scripzure; it assumes that God does not know what He is doing in allowing the circumstances of life to fall in on us. Faith and self-pity cannot coexist because faith believes, "And we know that God causes all things to work together for good to those who love God, to those who are called according to His purpose" (Rom. 8:28).

Faith believes that God is near us even when we are abused, misunderstood, or rejected. Faith has confidence that God will some day bring to light all the details of every situation, and then justice will be meted out.

And it is precisely this kind of faith that also produces praise. As Scripture says, "He who offers a sacrifice of thanksgiving honors Me; and to him who orders his way aright I shall show the salvation of God" (Psalm 50:23). I've known believers who have been delivered from depression through memorizing psalms of praise that they would quote to God when those dark moments settled upon them. Any demonic forces that would want to exploit the emotion of depression or guilt are repelled when we cultivate a life of constant thanksgiving. God wants us to thank Him for the heartaches as well as the successes that we encounter. Through our faith and praise, His name is honored regardless of our circumstances.

David learned that gladness follows forgiveness. Joy is the fruit of righteousness. Of course, I'm not saying that we must always live with emotional tranquility. Christ didn't, nor need we. We all have our ups and downs—sometimes more of the former than the latter. We are to walk by faith, not emotional supports. But depression, that great heaviness of spirit marked by continual passivity, regret, and despair, can be conquered by choosing to do the will of God. That means we accept His cleansing, forgive others, and be obedient to whatever God requires. Unlike Judas and Saul, David discovered that the answer to his depression was found in the mercy of God.

Suggested Application

1. What factors may have caused a man of God like Elijah to experience such depression that he longed to die (1 Kings 19:4)?

2. God promised Israel fear and despondency if they would not obey Him (Deut. 28:65). What sins have we committed as a nation that may be contributing to the emotional malaise of this generation?

3. What did Christ do to enable Him to survive the emotional depression of Gethsemane (Matt. 26:36-

42)? Take particular note of His honesty and the role His friends were asked to have during those difficult hours.

4. In Psalm 77, Asaph expresses the deepest anguish of depression. But in the last half of the psalm, his spirit improves immeasurably. What made the difference?

5. In overcoming guilt, we must remember that we need not confess the same specific sin twice (unless, of course, we commit it again). Rather, we must learn to praise the Lord for His forgiveness. Find all the verses you can that assure us that our sins are forgiven and blotted out.

6. Study Job 1:1-2 to find out what caused Job's self-pity in chapter 3. How was Job's attitude eventually changed (chap. 42)?

5

Living with Rejection

DORIE HAD never known the love of a mother. Day after day she looked after her younger sister, hoping that her mother would recognize her and show her some affection. Yet even though her mother would cuddle her sister, tuck her into bed, and kiss her goodnight, she brushed off all of Dorie's attempts to win her mother's love.

One day, both Dorie and her sister were taken to an orphanage. Their mother visited them only twice in seven years. Eventually Dorie and her sister were placed in a foster home, where they were beaten and fed leftovers. From this couple, Dorie discovered that her mother was a waitress. One day, she and her sister set out to find their mother, going from cafe to cafe. At the end of the day they found her, only to be rudely rejected.

By the time she was eighteen, Dorie had been in many foster homes and had been so badly beaten that her back was sometimes a mass of welts and cuts. She had never heard anyone say, "I love you."

Dorie's example of rejection is not an isolated case, for as she today travels and speaks to women's groups, she is besieged by women and girls with similar experiences of deep rejection. One reason is the escalating divorce rate. Statistics show that one-half of all children born in the United States will at one point live with only one parent. Many not only feel that they have been rejected by one parent, but they also feel responsible for what has happened in their families. Often they have to sit through ugly and grueling court battles, seeing one parent reject the other—and them.

Unwanted children are another cause for rejection. They may have been conceived out of wedlock (as Dorie had been, she discovered later), or their parents really did not want children at all. From early childhood, these children sense that they are not wanted. They are pushed aside as an inconvenience, a nuisance. The most desperate attempts to gain attention only arouse anger and resentment in their parents. As the days drag by, the children sink deeper into rejection. Many become runaways, where they often become victims of those pandering to the sexual appetites of unscrupulous men and women.

Even in homes where children are accepted and loved, one or more may experience tacit rejection. The oldest child may be the most brilliant, and the parents begin to favor that child, making unfavorable comparisons that deeply wound the second child. Other parents favor the prettiest daughter, giving her special attention and privileges. The implicit rejection of the less intelligent, the less beautiful, causes deep feelings of rejection. These again may result in all kinds of special efforts to gain favorable attention. If these fail, such children may resort to negative behavior as a last resort to be seen and heard.

Rejection may come in adult life—and be just as traumatic. Ann had been married for twenty years and had spent her life raising the eight children the Lord had given her and her husband. Deeply religious, she saw that they all went to Sunday school regularly with her. Her husband was king in her life; he could do no wrong. Though she had been aware of some cooling in his ardor, she was unprepared when he told her he was getting a divorce and marrying his secretary. Devastated by this rejection, she eventually was admitted to a mental hospital. Two years after this rejection, she set out to take her own life.

Or consider Jim, who had been a highly successful businessman until his mid-forties. As vice president in charge of marketing, he exuded self-confidence. Then his company was merged with a much larger one. In the merger, he was forced out. Two years later he was still floundering, convinced he was doomed to be a failure. Repeated rejection in his attempt to find a new position robbed him of his self-confidence. The fact that his wife had to work to keep bread on the table only increased his feelings of guilt, rejection, and anger.

This feeling of rejection is the seedbed for a whole cluster of negative emotions. Rejected people usually feel terribly alone. Their loneliness can lead to depression, despair, and attempts at suicide. Or the person becomes indifferent and hard to those who have rejected him, saying in effect, "I don't care what you think. I am going to be indifferent toward you because you have wronged me." Children may simply disappear and never notify their parents where they have gone. Brothers and sisters refuse to show at family occasions where the other is present. Such bitterness may transfer to those on the job, so that the rejected person refuses to talk to fellow employees.

Frequently, rejection leads to demonic activity. I don't know of another emotion that is so often exploited by demonic powers. Overwhelmed by their rejection, people cannot seem to break out of their shells. They feel worthless, totally insecure, full of despair and hopelessness. Somehow, these feelings so color their thinking that they see no way out of their prison. Satan has them bound.

We read in Proverbs, "The spirit of a man can endure his sickness, but a broken spirit who can bear?" (Prov. 18:14). You and I can put up with bodily injury; you can break your leg and recover; you can experience many physical pains. Yet what happens when the spirit within you is wounded? The writer of Proverbs leaves it simply as a question, as though the answer is obvious. The emotionally wounded person cannot deal with feelings of rejection on the basis of the intellect alone. You can say, "I will reject them. I will refuse them. I will not think about them." But those emotional feelings stay in your subconscious and will surface constantly unless you deal with them at a deep level of consciousness.

If denying those feelings is not the way to deal with rejection, what is? I believe we will find the answer in a study of Isaiah 53. Based on the insights contained in this passage from God's Word, I believe it is possible for you, no matter what your background, to move from rejection to acceptance. You can move from self-pity to praise, from bitter feelings to feelings of love. God has made provision to heal those feelings of rejection.

Before you read any more, get your Bible and thoughtfully read Isaiah 53. Underline the words that express rejection and the resulting feelings. Then underline what Jesus, who is the focus of this chapter, has done for us despite the rejection He experienced. When you have done this, keep your Bible open beside you as you read the rest of this chapter.

First, I want you to notice that *Jesus Christ's rejection was complete.* In verse 2, Jesus is compared to a plant, a tender shoot that grows up out of parched ground. That is in contrast to someone who was brought up, as it were, in a well-watered garden. Jesus Christ, the Son of God, grew up in a society that rejected Him, in "parched ground."

Consider the lineage of Jesus. You'll find prostitutes and other notable sinners listed. Christ could hardly boast of His family tree! Beyond that, Jesus Christ was raised in the town of Nazareth so that He might be called a Nazarene (Matt. 2:23). The city of Nazareth was a despised city to the high society of that day. It was the ghetto of Israel, the wrong side of the tracks. That is why in the gospels, people referred to Jesus with derision as a Nazarene. He had the stigma of Nazareth, and that was one reason why He was rejected by society.

Jesus was also rejected by His peers. Notice that in verse 3 He is described as "rejected of men," or as we read in the *New American Standard Bible*, "He was despised and forsaken of men." He was a "man of sorrows, and acquainted with grief." Jesus Christ was ridiculed and mocked; they tried to push Him over the brow of a hill at one time. When He finally came to die, the Herodians and Sadducees, who could never agree on anything, decided to overlook their differences so they could unite against Jesus Christ.

How did Jesus bear that rejection? Did He take it stoically? Was it like water off a duck's back? The Bible clearly tells us that the answer is no. Already in the Old Testament prophecy in Isaiah 53, He was described as "a man of sorrows, and acquainted with grief."

Are you acquainted with grief? Do you rise in the morning with grief? Do you go to bed at night with grief? Jesus Christ was well-acquainted with grief. "He came to His own, and those who were His own did not receive Him" (John 1:11). His own people rejected Him, and because of that Jesus Christ received great heaviness of spirit. Even His friend Judas rejected Him and betrayed Him. So Jesus experienced the upheaval of emotions that you experience when you are rejected. In fact, we read that Jesus was of such heaviness of spirit that He was "like one from whom men hide their face" (v. 3). He was like a leper.

Have you ever seen someone who sorrows so much, and is under such heaviness of spirit, that you don't even want to look at him? That's the way Jesus was, the Bible says.

It is true that in the midst of this there was joy in doing the Father's will. Jesus did have this satisfaction in the middle of that rejection and hurt. It is important, however, to see clearly that Jesus Christ experienced the rejection of society and His peers. He knows what it is like to be abandoned.

By now you may be saying, "Yes, I agree that all this is true, but I have an even worse story to tell. Jesus Christ was accepted by His parents, Mary and Joseph, but I was rejected by my parents. Jesus Christ was never married, so He does not know what it is like to be rejected by a lover, a wife, or a husband."

Let me discuss a third form of rejection experienced by Jesus, a rejection more excruciating and difficult than any rejection experienced by you. Not only was He rejected by society, by His peers—but He was also rejected by God, His Father. Look at verse 4 of Isaiah 53: "Surely our griefs He Himself bore, and our sorrows He carried; yet we ourselves esteemed Him stricken, smitten of God, and afflicted." And in verse 10 we read, "But the LORD was pleased to crush Him." When Jesus died on the cross, He cried out, "My God, my God, why hast Thou forsaken me?" (Matt. 27:46). It was as if He were saying, "I can understand why men would forsake me, but, oh, my God, why hast *Thou* forsaken me?" He was abandoned by His Father.

You have to remember that Jesus Christ was God. He was the second Person of the Godhead. As such, He was making a payment for the sins of the world. That payment was to God. God was dying for God. That is a tremendous mystery; there is no mystery in theology as deep as the incarnation and the sacrificial death of Jesus Christ on the cross. Yet Jesus Christ knew in those moments on the cross what it was like to have the Father, with whom He had such fellowship, turn His back on Him, because at that point He became legally guilty of every sin that was ever committed. He became *legally* guilty of incest, genocide, adultery, lying, and stealing. Because of that, He died alone. Abandoned. It was the worst form of rejection you could ever experience.

Many of you may be feeling rejected because of some physical defect, real or imagined. You were not as beautiful, not as bright, not as obedient, not as talented. You can take heart: Jesus Christ, the sinless One, experienced deep rejection, too. That proves that your rejection is unrelated to your intrinsic worth as an individual. You are worth just as much as someone who grew up in a home where he or she was accepted. Get your pen and underline that sentence. *In the sight of God, in terms of your real value as a person, you are just as important, as worthy of acceptance, as any other person you know.*

Having established the complete nature of Christ's rejection, we move on to the second insight we can gain from Isaiah 53: *His rejection secured our acceptance.* That prophetic passage teaches us that Jesus Christ bore two things for us—at least two things. One is our sin. In verse 5 we read, "But He was pierced through for our transgressions, He was crushed for our iniquities." Note well, "The chastening for our well-being fell upon Him." And "by His scourging we are healed." That is possible because "the LORD has caused the iniquity of us all to fall on Him" (v. 6). The sinless Jesus, the truly perfect God-man, died in our place. Theologians refer to it as the substitutionary death of Jesus.

During the U.S. Civil War, a man who had lost his wife and had several children to care for was drafted. He did not want to go, so a young man in the community volunteered to go in his place. He was killed in the war. But as a result, the man with a family did not have to go to war. There was no way the government could force him to go into battle, because he had already gone in the person of the young man. Someone had taken his place. In the same way, Jesus Christ was hanged on the cross in our place. He bore our sins and transgressions, accepting the punishment due us for our sin.

Yet Jesus also bore something else, our negative emotions. Isaiah 53:4 clearly states, "Surely our griefs He Himself bore, and our sorrows He carried." Christ not only died that you could be forgiven and free from sin, but He also bore your sorrow, your rejection, and your hurt. Consequently, all of those ugly emotions that rise up within you to make you miserable may be carried away. As a result you can say, "Thank God, I am free."

Just imagine someone sitting down beside you as you are struggling with rejection and saying, "You know, I think you have borne those emotions too long. Why don't you give them to me. I'll carry them for you for a week. Maybe I'll give them back to you then, but I'll just take them home for a while." Wouldn't it be nice if after the week the person did not want to give them back to you? He would simply say, "I'll bear them for you." You could be free!

Jesus Christ did just that for you. He was hanged on the cross. He experienced all those rejections and sorrows, those hurts and the abandonment by God, so that you would not have to endure them anymore. Yes, Jesus Christ took upon Himself our sins *and* our sorrows and ugly feelings.

That does not mean that we will never sorrow, that we will never have any bad emotions. Sometimes we do have them. An analogy is the biblical truth that Jesus Christ tasted death for every man. That doesn't mean that we die to our humanity. What it means is that our sorrow can be turned into joy as we understand that He becomes our Burdenbearer because He died in our place.

It is important that we recognize the significance of Jesus Christ's substitutionary death. Examine Isaiah 53:11: "As a result of the anguish of His soul, He will see it and be satisfied; by His knowledge the Righteous One, My Servant, will justify the many, as He will bear their iniquities." Inasmuch as all our sins were placed upon Jesus Christ, and He died for our sin, all of Jesus Christ's righteousness is now imputed to us. We really have made an exchange, and we certainly got a good deal! Jesus Christ says, "I will receive all your sins." In return, He transfers to us His righteousness.

This is why the Bible says that believers are highly favored of the Lord. It is not a case of God's beginning to tolerate you, saying in effect, "Now I can put up with you." No! The Bible clearly teaches that you are highly favored of the Lord, accepted in the Beloved. All the wonderful thoughts God has toward His Son are now directed to every believer. After spending so much and sacrificing His Son for you, you are now number one on God's list of priorities in the universe!

There is a third insight you'll need to overcome rejection: *Just as God has now accepted you, you will have to accept others.* This is not explicitly stated in Isaiah 53, but it is very clear from Ephesians 4:32: "And be kind to one another, tender-hearted, forgiving each other, just as God in Christ also has forgiven you."

You say, "How does our acceptance before God enable us to forgive one another?" To begin with, our acceptance in the sight of God enables us to accept ourselves. During my ministry I have met scores, if not hundreds, of people who have tremendously negative thoughts about themselves. Psychologists call it a bad self-image. These people really believe that they are just awful, that they are failures. Deep inside of them, they consider themselves worthless. This feeling about themselves runs roughshod over their emotional responses, forcing them to actually believe these things about themselves.

If you are one of those, I want you to know that you are not worth any less than any other human being. We are all of equal value in the sight of God, with whom there is no respect of persons. Your emotions are not an accurate gauge of your value.

Once you begin to see that you are accepted by God, you can say, "Lord, I thank You that You have created me. I thank You that I am alive. I thank You that You have accepted me. If You can love me and accept me just as I am, I will accept my appearance, I will accept my background, I will accept my lack of education. I will accept any negative thing that has come to me and I will say thank You, God, because one thing is sure: I am accepted and highly beloved in the sight of the Lord God." As David put it, "For my father and my mother have forsaken me, but the LORD will take me up" (Psalm 27:10).

Next, you must choose to forgive those who have wronged you. You may not feel like forgiving, but forgiveness is not an emotion. Forgiving is an act of obedience dependent on the will.

Consider the child who grows up in a home where he is rejected. One of the things he says is, "If it's the last thing I do, I'll get my parents to accept me." He works hard and is often obedient. He may do all kinds of little extra things, looking for recognition and acceptance. Unfortunately, parents are sometimes so filled with selfishness that they are unable to accept their child even with that. And if the child does achieve acceptance, it may be only temporary, based on a specific performance. That's why if your parents have rejected you and you are now an adult, the chances of your finally being accepted by them are small. It may happen, and I know of one case where it did, but only rarely. The answer to your problem is not to say, "I will do anything to receive their acceptance." If you do, it can hurt your relationship with your husband or wife, damage your relationship with your children—and you merely perpetuate the rejection through another generation. You must reach the point where you simply say, "I choose to forgive them." And if your parents or your mate are dead? That does not matter, since you are not only doing it for their sake. I am asking you to do it for your sake. Forgiveness is a favor you are doing yourself. Just as God has forgiven you because He chose to, you can choose to forgive a parent, a husband or wife (even an ex-husband or wife), and children who may have rejected you. I have heard of people having to go to graves and pour out their emotions so that they can finally and irrevocably choose to forgive.

Feelings are tricky. Emotions are affected by many things. So even if you have prayed to God and accepted His assessment of your worth in Christ, and even if you have deliberately chosen to forgive the one who has rejected you, the feelings may return. How do you overcome them?

You can take three steps to overcome feelings of rejection. The first is to begin a life of praise. This has to become a priority. You must consistently praise the Lord because you have been accepted and highly favored of the Lord. Every day, read a Psalm or two that focuses on praise to God. Thank Him for the acceptance that is secure, immovable, and not dependent upon your performance. Memorize verses of praise that can be repeated when the feelings of rejection start surfacing.

Second, you must lay down all bitterness. Simply say, "Even though it hurts, and every emotion in my body militates against it, by God's grace I choose to forgive and accept the fact that Jesus bore my rejection for me so that I can be free."

Then, take the risk of making new friendships. You no longer need to be withdrawn, determined never to be hurt again. You will begin to open your life to others, making yourself vulnerable to them because you know your security ultimately does not rest in man but in God. He accepts you today just as He accepts His Son.

You have read this far and in your mind you have been saying, "That's right, but I'm afraid to get started because I might fail." God accepts even your failure. He does not reject you even after a dozen false starts. It is not three strikes and you are out. Right now you can pray the following prayer as your start.

Dear Father, I thank You that Jesus Christ died on my behalf. I thank You that He bore not only my sin but also my sorrows. I thank You that He experienced deep rejection, and I am glad that He can identify with me. Right now I want to make the substitution; I want to make the exchange. I choose to forgive the one(s) who have wronged me. I accept Jesus Christ's help in doing so. And because I am now highly favored, I thank You for my gifts, my limitations, and my abilities. I thank You again that I was born, and I thank You that today I can be free. Finally, because I am highly favored, I thank You that I can love others in the energy of the risen Christ. Amen.

Suggested Application

1. Based on Psalm 118:22, how did God use Christ's rejection for an ultimate good?

2. Although being rejected by our parents or friends is severe, contemplate for a moment what it would be like to be rejected by God (Matt. 8:12; Rev. 20:11-15).

3. Perhaps the best antidote to feelings of depression is to be secure in the love and acceptance of God. Memorize these promises of assurance that will focus on this relationship (Deut. 32:10; Eph. 1:3-6; 1 Pet. 2:9).

4. Feelings of depression can only be overcome by a daily life of praise. Read a Psalm of praise each day to God. Honor Him by expressing worship through your lips (e.g., Psalms 103; 145-50).

6

When Fear Envelops You

HAVE YOU ever heard someone make one of the following statements?

"I'll never drive a car in Chicago. Never! That kind of traffic scares me to death."

"I won't go with you to the banquet. I'm scared I will make a fool of myself in front of those wealthy, sophisticated people."

"Don't ever ask me to say something in public. I'd be so scared that I would forget everything I wanted to say."

Or consider what a woman told me last week: "Because of a past relationship with a man, I've lived in fear for five years, afraid he'll come to the door or kill me when I go outside. So I lock myself upstairs when I'm home alone."

Fear. The kind of fear that can paralyze, that can prevent you from enjoying life, that can lock up deep inside the gifts that God has given you, never to be used.

Some fears are normal and actually for our benefit. You are driving along the expressway and are momentarily distracted by a sign or the car next to you. When your eyes refocus on the roadway ahead of you, a car is entering your lane from the other side, cutting you off.

A shiver of fear runs up your spine as your foot jumps onto the brake pedal.

Or you are walking with a friend down a city sidewalk. You are in a deep conversation as you approach an intersection. As you step down to the street, out of the corner of your eye you see a car approaching. With a jerk you stop and get back on the sidewalk, and as you do so a quick skip of your heartbeat reminds you that fear caused you to stop before you got out into traffic.

This kind of fear motivates you to take the children into the basement of your house when you hear that a tornado may be coming. It causes you to warn your children about the danger of playing with matches and the danger of stopping to talk to strangers.

There is a third kind of fear, a fear for which there is no logical reason. Irrational fear makes no sense to the onlooker—and usually doesn't make sense to the one afraid, either. Some people, for example, are afraid of crowds. They are fine one-on-one, but as soon as a group gathers in their area, they start to feel uncomfortable. When you ask them why they are afraid of a crowd, they cannot explain it. Others, of course, are more comfortable in a crowd and are terrified at the idea of having to talk to someone one-on-one unless they know him very well.

Some people are afraid of marriage. Others are afraid they will lose their jobs and live with their fear year in and year out. You may be one of those afraid to go home because you keep wondering what might have happened in your absence.

Whatever your fear, the first thing you need to remember is that God created you with the capacity to fear. He built that emotional response within you just as surely as He gave you the ability to love and respond warmly to other people. Fear is part of His loving provision for us. Properly controlled, fear can protect us from harm, and it can motivate us to positive action. Uncontrolled fear, however, can put us into a personal prison and stunt our personal and spiritual growth.

This chapter is designed to help you understand and control your fear. I want to help you push back the walls of the prison that fear has built for you so that you can go free.

At this point you may be saying, "I don't really want to do that. I built that wall myself to protect me from hurt. I laid a very careful and deep foundation. I built the walls sky high and am determined to live behind those walls."

You may be like some people I know. They are afraid to have company in their home. For twenty-five years they've lived in their lovely home and never invited anyone over, not even for coffee. They are afraid the water might not boil, that the cake won't turn out right, that their company won't like their living room decor. Something is bound to go wrong if they ever open that front door to others. These fears are the walls they won't push aside. In fact, their fears have become their security blanket that they hug to their bosom as tightly as Linus carries his blanket with him.

The apostle Paul has a message for you. He wrote to Timothy, "For God hath not given us the spirit of fear" (2 Tim. 1:7, KJV). And the apostle John reminded us that "perfect love casts out fear" (1 John 4:18). You can be free from the bondage of fear. Fear need not control your actions.

The paralyzing effect of fear is illustrated by one of the incidents in Jesus' life, related in Matthew 14:22-31. Jesus had just fed the five thousand men, plus women and children. The crowd was thinning out when He asked the disciples to get into a boat and head for the other side of the lake, where He would meet them. He went up into the mountain to pray.

When the boat was about four miles from shore, a storm sprang up. The wind buffeted the little boat, and the waves began pounding against the side of it. Inasmuch as many of the disciples were fishermen, this was no new experience even though it was very dangerous, but what they saw coming across the water was definitely not normal. Walking toward them *on the water* was the figure of a man. The Scriptures record: "And when the disciples saw Him walking on the sea, they were frightened, saying, 'It is a ghost!' And they cried out for fear" (v. 26). Sound like a tough group of fishermen?

The experience of these disciples points to the first step in demolishing the walls of fear—*you must see your fear in perspective.* Matthew reported that Jesus came to those disciples, and they thought that He was a ghost. They had a fear of the storm based on experience, but their greater fear came from perceiving Jesus' figure as a ghost.

That reaction is not unusual even today. There are many who believe that when a person dies, his spirit might return to traverse the earth, haunting different places and people. You and I know this is not true; yes, there are spirits that do haunt certain people and places, but those are not human spirits. They are evil, demonic spirits. The disciples were not that spiritually perceptive yet, so when their superstitious minds focused on the advancing figure, they naturally assumed it was a ghost. They could not relate this experience to anything that had ever happened to them before, as they had never seen anyone walk on water. Only after the initial outcry caused by fear did anyone even dream that it was Jesus who was the object of their fear.

What can you learn from this about your perspective on fear? You must see that *Jesus is in the midst of your fear*. Fear has a way of distorting our perception, and we don't see and understand the true object of our fears, but wrapped up in that object are the loving arms and concern of Jesus Christ.

Dr. Harry Ironside used to tell a story about himself that also illustrates this point. He would pretend that he was a bear. He would get on his hands and knees and chase his son around the room, all the while growling like a bear. The little boy would become fearful and be really frightened at first. Then one day when the little boy was backed into a corner, he suddenly turned and rushed into his father's arms. "You're not a bear, you're my papa!" he said.

From that incident, Dr. Ironside learned an important lesson: Often the experience we fear the most is actually an act of God. He is attempting to put His arms around us. That's why I can say with full assurance that Jesus is in the midst of your fear. The misinterpretation, the misunderstanding, that has come to you as a result of that fear can be dissipated when you realize that Jesus Christ is in the midst of it—just as He was in the midst of the disciples' fear.

There is something else you must understand if you are to get the proper perspective on your fear. *Not only is Jesus Christ in the midst of your fear, but Jesus also knows what your fear is all about and the feelings it gives you.*

When Jesus came to the disciples during the fourth watch at night, He said to them, "Take courage, it is I; do not be afraid" (v. 27). I particularly like the line in the first part of the verse: "But immediately Jesus spoke to them." He recognized their fear and immediately set about allaying it.

What had tipped off Jesus that the disciples were

afraid? Had He overheard their cry of fear? No, I'm convinced that He knew it because He is the Son of God and He knew what was troubling their hearts. There just was no way their voices could have reached Him during the high wind.

As you read this, what fear is uppermost in your mind? What is the fear that possibly keeps you awake for part of the night, that limits your effectiveness on the job, that hampers your service for Christ? Name it—and then know that Jesus knew all along that it was there in your heart and occupying your mind.

God knew all about the fear that would consume you when He inserted the message "Fear not" more than one hundred times in the Bible. You ask, "Why one hundred times? Wouldn't once be enough?" Those of you who are parents of preschool children probably know why. My wife and I, at least, have had to tell our children some things at least one hundred times! Why? Because my wife and I have learned that sometimes even ninety-nine times are not enough. And God said "Fear not" over one hundred times because He knows what is going on inside you, and He knows that when we are paralyzed by fear we don't hear very well.

Before we go on to the second step in overcoming our fears, let's summarize the first: To deal with fear, you must get a proper perspective on your fear, and that happens only when you recognize that Jesus is in the midst of it and knows all about your fear. This then leads us to the second step—*you must have the right focus during your fear if you are to get help.*

Let's examine Peter's experience with Christ. Jesus said as He approached the boat, "It is I." To this Peter quickly responded, "Lord, if it is You, command me to come to You on the water" (v. 28). He was ready for a quick test of the authenticity of that voice and Person.

Some people are like that. They are never sure whether God means what He says, and they always want to test it out. That can be dangerous, for the Bible says, "You shall not put the LORD your God to the test" (Deut. 6:16). Yet in this instance, Peter did risk the test and say, "If it is You"—implying that he wasn't quite sure yet—"command me to come to You on the water."

Jesus said, "Come!"

When Jesus said that word, Peter should have rested in the absolute assurance from the Lord Himself that he could make it to His Master. Jesus wasn't about to say "Come" and let Peter sink. Yet Peter's focus shifted from Jesus to the wind, and that resulted in more fear despite the invitation from the Lord Himself.

Our focus should never be on circumstances. When Peter began walking on the water, he was on solid ground with the Lord. The Bible says he "came toward Jesus," implying his eyes were on Jesus (v. 29). When his eyes shifted focus and saw the waves, he didn't see only the waves but also the wind that was so boisterous. At that moment, "he became afraid" and began to sink (v. 30).

Like a lot of us, Peter had within him the alternating spirits of fear and trust. When he looked at the Lord, he trusted. When he looked at the circumstances in which he was with the Lord, he became afraid. The shift in focus to the circumstances brought on fear because it caused doubt to arise in his mind about his ability to negotiate the distance between himself and Jesus. That word *doubt* means to try to go both ways, and that was what Peter was trying to do, go both ways.

Instead of focusing on the circumstances, your focus must be on the promises of God. Jesus had in effect promised Peter that he would be able to walk on the water and make it all the way to Jesus. Peter should have focused on that promise and kept walking, regardless of the activity of the wind and waves. He did not do it and started sinking as fear of the wind took hold in his heart.

Focusing on the promises of God means that we are obedient to the call of God in them. We choose to obey despite the fears that might arise from circumstances. Let's suppose your problem is fear of crowds. You simply feel uncomfortable as soon as more than half a dozen people are gathered together. Let's further suppose you are paralyzed by that fear. Determined to overcome that fear, no matter what, you decide to go into that crowd, saying inside yourself, "I will overcome this fear, I will overcome this fear." Do you think fear will flee as the crowd begins engulfing you?

Certainly not, because your whole focus is on your fear, and the minute you get into that crowd, that fear will again come upon you. It will arise like the mist at dawn and envelope your heart, and you'll rush out of that crowd, totally defeated.

On the other hand, your focus can be on obedience. You can say to yourself, "God in His Word has commanded me to get together with His people, and this fear is hindering me from doing that. So I will focus on Jesus Christ and His promises and move in obedience to Him. If I happen to become afraid in a crowd, and I'm hoping I won't, I will simply have to live with it. I will accept it because it has happened before and I have lived through it. Thus I will be obedient regardless of my feelings of fear." If you do that, you will soon discover that your attention will shift away from your fears. Soon you will be able to be in crowds, preoccupied with your responsibility to interact with others and love them as Christ commanded. In time, those fears will not trouble you anymore.

The reason for this is both psychological and spiritual. The psychological reason is that when we focus on the very thing we are trying to be rid of, its power over us actually increases. In this case, fear becomes a self-fulfilling prophecy. If you focus on how afraid you are, you will soon discover that you are very much afraid—indeed, your fear will grow stronger. But if your focus is on Jesus and on your obedience to Him, His power will flow through your whole being and help drive away the fear.

If Peter had kept his eyes on Jesus, he would have been able to walk across the Atlantic Ocean as long as Jesus had said, "Come." The Bible teaches that perfect love casts out fear, and the reason it does is that your love for God and His promises transcends the fear and overcomes that crippling force in your spiritual life.

Consider the woman who is afraid of dogs. One day when she hears a dog snarl, she remembers that her one-year-old son is outside playing. Without a doubt she will rush outside, grab the child, and run back inside even if the dog comes at her. Her love is stronger than her fear. How much more is loving obedience to God able to overcome paralyzing fear!

I truly feel sorry for people who live in a constant state of fear. They are forever taking their spiritual temperature to see how much fear they happen to have today. Their focus on their fear only increases it. Throw away the thermometer and begin basking in the glow of God's warm love, for it will cast out fear.

Yet the experience of Peter and the disciples that night reminds us of another step in overcoming fear. To be truly victorious over fear, you need not only a proper perspective on your fear and a proper focus in your fear, *but you also need a proper faith.*

Notice what Jesus did when Peter cried out in his

fear, "Lord, save me!" He stretched out His hand and took hold of Peter before he had gone down very far. Then He said, "O you of little faith, why did you doubt?" (v. 31). He pointedly referred to the real reason for Peter's failure, his lack of faith in Jesus Christ.

Let me remind you of three things that are involved in proper faith. First, you must recognize that God ordains fearful circumstances. "Hold it," you're saying, "run that by me again." OK, why were the disciples in the boat in the middle of a dangerous storm at the fourth watch of the night? *They were there because Jesus had told them to get into the boat and cross the lake ahead of Him.* They received explicit instructions and obeyed Him implicitly, yet despite that they found themselves in the middle of a storm.

As lovingly as I can, let me remind you that the smoothest path in life is not always the most holy path. Sometimes the most holy path is the roughest path. Some of you are probably saying, "Right on. I gave up my job for Jesus Christ. I could be earning more money, but I believe God has called me into a ministry for Him. So now we are making less money and are starting to have problems in our family. We are experiencing health problems on top of everything, even though we believe we obeyed God." That was exactly the experience of Jesus' disciples—circumstances were difficult even though they were doing the will of God!

Jesus wants you to understand that no matter how severe the storm, it is God-ordained. And because He ordained it, He is there in it with you. Once you recognize that, you will, like the disciples, worship in reverence and in awe at the power that is active in your life.

But God not only ordains fearful circumstances; we can be grateful that He also monitors them—that is, He keeps close watch on how we are faring in the midst of the storms of life. Although the disciples couldn't see Christ when the storm began, He could see them! Isn't that true of our experience? Often we wonder where Christ is or whether He has lost interest in our predicament, but He is on the sidelines, watching the whole ordeal. And when push comes to shove as it so often does in life, I would prefer that Christ see me rather than that I see Him!

Christ carefully monitored the situation and came to them in their distress. He calculated the best time to come to them personally. It happened to be 3 A.M., the darkest hour of the night. No sooner nor any later did Christ choose to make His appearance. The disciples, exhausted by the storm and frustrated by Christ's apparent indifference to their plight, had come to the end of their rope—Christ met them there (and calmed the storm [v. 32], even though His appearance was initially more frightening than the storm).

Where are you in your battle with fear? Is the evening turning to darkness, or is the darkness already beginning to blend into the morning light? Wherever, I want you to remember that Christ is near, taking inventory of your situation and available when you turn to Him. His timing is perfect, His love intense. The psalmist wrote, "I sought the LORD, and He answered me, and delivered me from all my fears" (Psalm 34:4). Like the disciples, this man came to worship the God who delivered him from his fears.

Let me be clear: Learning to focus on God's promises in faith does not mean that God will always change the fearful circumstances. Sometimes the storms of life continue; often those fearful situations rear their ugly heads once again. But though the circumstances might not change, we will. We will live without those paralyzing fears that rob us of our Christian freedom.

Finally, in the Scriptures there is a direct connection between God's presence and the absence of fear. For example, Hebrews 13:5 implies that we can be free from the fear of poverty and the fear of men by remembering that God is with us: "Let your character be free from the love of money, being content with what you have; for He Himself has said, 'I will never desert you, nor will I ever forsake you,' so that we confidently say, 'The LORD is my Helper, I will not be afraid. What shall man do to me?' " We can be content with our possessions and free from the fear of men because God will never abandon us. We've always got Him beside us.

The circumstances that we fear remind me of the walls in a penitentiary in British Columbia, Canada. When the structure was being demolished, the workmen discovered something interesting. Though the gates were steel and the windows were barred, the outer walls were made only of woodboard covered with clay and paper, painted to look as if the walls were thick metal. Anyone could have gone through those walls with little effort, but no prisoner ever tried it—they all believed the walls could never budge.

You will find that your fears are much the same; the walls you have built may appear formidable. You may even feel comfortable in your prison and find the thought of freedom frightening.

But today, you can push down those walls in the name of Jesus Christ. In your fears you can see the face of Jesus Christ disguised; you can choose to memorize God's promises rather than catering to your fluctuating emotions. You can accept the storms of life as God's will, His plan for strengthening your faith. You can join Peter in stepping out of the boat and walking with Christ. The circumstances that threaten to be over your head will suddenly be under your feet!

You'll have the exhilaration of stepping onto a cloud and discovering that your feet are on solid rock. Christ has already conquered your fears. Are you ready to accept His victory?

Suggested Application

1. What consequences may fear have in a person's life? (Lev. 26:36; Matt. 26:69-75; 28:4; Luke 21:26; John 9:22; 19:12-16)?

2. Notice how our fear of man should be replaced by our fear of God (Psalm 27:1; Prov. 10:27; Matt. 10:26-31). Why are the two kinds of fear mutually exclusive?

3. If it is never God's will for us to be overcome with fear (2 Tim. 1:7), what might be the source of our fears? What did God do for David (Psalm 34:4)?

4. Satan often exploits our fears, telling us we must live in our private prisons. Why do we have authority to command our fears to leave us (read Eph. 1:15—2:6)?

5. Think of all the fears you have had that were unfounded. How can we prevent such a waste of nervous energy in the future (1 Pet. 5:7)?

6. Perhaps man's greatest fear is the fear of death. What can we learn from Christ and Paul about how to approach the experience (Luke 23:46; John 13:1-5; 2 Tim. 4:6-8)? Find other passages that tell us how believers have faced death in the past—Stephen, for example.

7

Sure Cure for Loneliness

ONE OF the most persistent themes in American music has been the feeling of loneliness. Whether sung by the trapper in front of his open fire in the wilderness, the cowboy loping across the prairie on his horse, or the man strumming his guitar in front of the fireplace, popular songs have consistently majored on loneliness. This loneliness might be caused by a broken relationship, unrequited love, or distance from loved ones. Recently, loneliness has also become a major theme of Christian books, as we suddenly realized that our big cities are filled with lonely people and our current divorce rate is plunging a large, new segment of our population into intense loneliness.

The intensity of this loneliness is illustrated by a man in Chicago who wrote a letter to a reporter, saying that he was considering suicide. Shortly after mailing the letter, the man walked into a telephone booth and shot himself. When the letter arrived, the reporter discovered that the reason for the suicide was the untimely death in a fire of a five-year-old daughter and the subsequent death of his wife. He wrote that he planned to die because he could not stand the loneliness anymore.

This loneliness caused by bereavement is most severe when a husband or wife dies after several decades of marriage. Every piece of furniture in every room reminds the survivor of the loss suffered and sharply intensifies the loneliness. Some people feel God is unjust to let them stay alive when their life's partner is gone.

The individualism so rampant in America produces a second kind of loneliness, the loneliness of rejection. It's the feeling a wife may have if her husband comes home from work, gulps his food in silence, and settles into the easy chair in front of the television set. More and more children are also inflicting the loneliness of rejection on their parents. It is because of rejection that someone can feel lonely in a crowd.

When I visited a nursing home several years ago, I asked one of the supervisors, "How many of the residents of this home are visited by relatives at least several times a year?" She said that only about 30 percent receive such visits. Seventy percent have no one to visit them, even at Christmas.

One woman I know was so rejected by her two daughters that they had not contacted her in ten years. When she called them, they hung up on her. She told me that she finally took down all the pictures of them and threw them into the wastebasket. "I tried to convince myself that I never even had children," she said. But that is not possible. Whenever I visited her, she would talk about those two daughters and the loneliness they caused her.

I do not think there is anything more lonely than the loneliness of imminent death. I think of young men on the field of battle who know they are dying and have no one with them in those final hours. I see people in the hospital who are surrounded by all kinds of life-support equipment yet know they are going to die. Their relatives also know it, but they all studiously avoid the subject. The person in the bed finally realizes he will literally die alone.

People will do all kinds of things to escape loneliness. Witness the proliferation of singles bars, discotheques, and singles communities. One of the more creative approaches was by a man who went to a psychiatrist and asked for a split personality. At least that way he would have someone to live with!

The Bible records the example of a lonely man who discovered the sure cure for loneliness. I believe we can draw some helpful insights for overcoming loneliness from that experience, recorded in Genesis 28. Beginning with verse 10, we have the description of what may well have been Jacob's first night away from home after he stole the blessing from Esau.

That night under the open sky had all the potential for being an excruciatingly lonely experience. Jacob had left home that morning with at least two things on his mind, guilt over what he had done to his brother, Esau, and the realization that he would be separated from his mother for a long time. He was his mother's favorite son, and now he was leaving her with his aged and blind father, Isaac, and a vengeful Esau.

As he set out on the journey to Haran, the home of close relatives who would take him in while he waited for his brother's anger to subside, Jacob undoubtedly began to wonder if God would really give him the blessing his father had given him by mistake. Maybe he would have to make it without God. As the third generation in a family God had promised to bless abundantly, that was undoubtedly a most disturbing thought.

As night settled in on that rugged terrain, Jacob found a smooth stone that could serve as a pillow. It has been said that a hard pillow, an uneasy conscience, and a heavy heart are the sort of combination that makes one dream. Yet Jacob's dream came from a different source, for the Bible reports, "Behold, a ladder was set on the earth with its top reaching to heaven; and behold, the angels of God were ascending and descending on it. And behold, the Lord stood above it and said, 'I am the LORD, the God of your father Abraham and the God of Isaac; the land on which you lie, I will give it to you and to your descendants' " (Gen. 28:12-13). That dream became the vehicle God used to enter the consciousness of Jacob. Through it, Jacob became keenly aware of the presence of God.

The first truth God impressed on Jacob was that *God is a trustworthy Father*. In the context of Jacob's recent experience, this was a vital truth: "I am the God of your father Abraham and the God of Isaac."

God had made certain commitments to both Abraham and Isaac. We call them promises even though they were in the nature of a one-way covenant; the Almighty God committed Himself to future blessings upon the descendants of Abraham and Isaac. Now that Abraham was dead and an estranged Isaac was being left behind in a tent, Jacob could well have wondered about the continuing validity of God's commitments. God erased any doubt Jacob might have had. There is something truly wonderful about the concept God repeated to Jacob: "I was with your grandfather, I am with your father, and I will be with you." That is the word of a God who has continuity, a continuity that became effective for us in Jesus Christ.

God's commitment to Jacob contained three promises. The first was the promise of a rich inheritance: "The land on which you lie, I will give it to you and to your descendants" (v. 13). Think of it—God was saying to Jacob, "You are not washed up just because of your eagerness to grasp the blessing for yourself. When you walked across the fields and clambered over the rocks today, you may not have felt as though this would be your home some day. But it will be, because I have said so."

The theme of our inheritance as believers was picked up by the apostle Peter when he wrote, "To obtain an inheritance which is imperishable and undefiled and will not fade away, reserved in heaven for you, who are protected by the power of God through faith for a salvation ready to be revealed in the last time" (1 Pet. 1:4-5). God is as bound to the promises He has made to us as He had bound Himself to the promises made to Abraham, Isaac, and Jacob. Jesus referred to that when He prayed, "Father, I desire that they also, whom Thou hast given Me, be with Me where I am, in order that they may behold My glory, which Thou hast given Me" (John 17:24). We can expect God to fulfill that desire by His Son. You never need worry about new leadership annulling the covenant, for God will remain in control from eternity to eternity. He is a trustworthy Father who keeps His promises even to the lonely person.

Yet the promise God gave to Jacob was not restricted to him alone. God extended the promise to Jacob's descendants, even though Jacob was still unmarried and had no immediate prospects for a wife. That assured Jacob of a long-range future and tied God into whatever would happen to Jacob and his descendants in coming years. God would be there to fulfill His promise. Not only would God be there to dispel loneliness, but so would an abundance of children.

If you are a parent, know that God has given us promises that we can claim in connection with our children. Parents often do not realize their God-given responsibility before God of being priests in their households and claiming the children for Jesus Christ. Sometimes we have to take back the ground that the children may give to the enemy, but we must see that the God who is our God is also the God of our children.

God not only promised Jacob an inheritance and a multitude of descendants who would possess that inheritance, but He also promised to provide personal guidance. Look at Genesis 28:15: "And behold, I am with you, and will keep you wherever you go, and will bring you back to this land; for I will not leave you until I have done what I have promised you."

It is clear that Jacob was traveling alone. He was defenseless against attack by a marauding band of desert dwellers. He had no guide to show him the best route to take. When he got to his destination, he would be among strangers, even though they were his relatives. With that prospect ahead of him, the promise of God that He would keep Jacob wherever he would go was most reassuring.

This is the God who comes to you in your loneliness today. He is aware of the pain of separation from loved ones, the loneliness of not knowing what the future holds. He is even aware of the guilt you are trying to deny. And He comes to you and says, "Behold, I am with you."

God's promises are great affirmations that ring in the soul in the blackest hours of loneliness. Yet for you and me, God goes one step further, as He did for Jacob. He reminded Jacob that *He is an ever present companion.* Jacob recognized this when he awoke and said, "Surely the LORD is in this place, and I did not know it" (v. 16). Just saying it was such an overwhelming and scary thing that he continued, "How awesome is this place!

This is none other than the house of God, and this is the gate of heaven" (v. 17).

Through this experience, God brought home two realities to Jacob. One is that God is near. We tend to think that God visited Jacob in a dream and then left him to sleep through the rest of the night. Not so. God was always there; He is omnipresent, everywhere at the same time. In fact, God was there long before Jacob found the stone for his pillow, as Jacob recognized after the dream.

The apostle Paul, speaking to the crowd assembled on Mars Hill, reminded them, "For in Him we live and move and exist" (Acts 17:28). That's just how close God is to you today.

What about non-Christians, you ask? Is God with them as well? Absolutely! In Daniel, chapter 5, there is the story of the wicked King Belshazzar, who brought into his drinking hall the sacred vessels from the Temple in Jerusalem. The activities of that night were also less than godly. Yet when Daniel was brought before the king, he said to Belshazzar, "The God in whose hand thy breath is, and whose are all thy ways, hast thou not glorified" (Dan. 5:23, KJV). God was just that close to Belshazzar, and he did not know it.

Why did Jacob not recognize that God was close to him until after the dream? I believe it was because of his moral failure. Whenever we have a sense of guilt, God seems so far away. Suddenly we say to ourselves, "Where is God?" We begin to search for Him as if He were a hidden treasure, when in reality He is right beside us all the time. He is as close to you as your breath, for it is in Him that we live and move and have our being. No matter how sinful you feel, no matter how far away from God you feel, the fact is that He is near.

That is one side of the coin. The other is that God is holy. Notice that Jacob said, "How awesome is this place! This is none other than the house of God, and this is the gate of heaven" (Gen. 28:17). He was so overcome with awe at the presence of God that he was afraid. Why? Because he realized he was a sinner. The thought of being in the presence of a holy God in the light of the sin he had just committed overwhelmed him. In his confusion, he may have thought that he somehow stumbled across the place where God was, into a localized manifestation. Once he walked on, he would wander out of the sphere of God's manifestation.

The recognition of God's holiness may make us feel that God is not going with us. We do not sense God's presence because we are out of tune with the Almighty, and our guilt and failure stands, as it were, as a barrier between us and a holy God. Yet the separation is not physical or geographical; rather, it is moral.

I sometimes liken this moral separation to radio waves. We cannot see them or feel them. Yet they totally fill the air around us. In fact, they are in us. Yet we do not become aware of the radio waves until we tune in a transistor radio that translates them into a wavelength we can hear. In the same way, God is with you, beside you, but you may not always be in fellowship with Him. You may be on a different frequency.

How do you get on His wavelength? The Bible is very clear about that. As we confess our sins, He is faithful and just to forgive us and cleanse us from all sin, reestablishing the fellowship (1 John 1:9). We may not immediately feel it, but we can accept this by faith and act upon it, because He has said He will never leave us or forsake us.

Have you ever considered a lonely hospital room to be the gate of heaven? It can be. This came home to me vividly when I visited Dr. William Culbertson, the president of Moody Bible Institute for many years. I was with him only once for a few precious moments, yet I sensed the presence of God. When I stopped at the nurses' station on my way out, they said, "When you go into that man's room, it is as if you are walking into the presence of God." Yes, despite all its loneliness and the terrifying consequences of being in it, the hospital room can become the house of God, the gate of heaven.

You may be one of those single folk who go home to an apartment each night in a large city. Most apartment buildings are not neighborly communities, so you may feel terribly alone as you step into your room. Remember, God is there with you—He has turned that room into the gate of heaven. And because He is a trustworthy Father and an ever present companion, you do not really need to let loneliness get you down.

Yet you may be like Jacob. He knew he was onto a good thing and wanted to get maximum benefit out of it. As a "schemer," he was always after a good bargain. To put himself in a good bargaining position, he made a vow: "If God will be with me and will keep me on this journey that I take, and will give me food to eat and garments to wear, and I return to my father's house in safety, then the LORD will be my God. And this stone, which I have set up as a pillar, will be God's house; and of all that Thou dost give me I will surely give a tenth to Thee" (Gen. 28:20-22). You will notice that he put all the things he wanted God to do up front, making sure that God knew what His end of the bargain was before he made any commitment to God.

How like us! God has given us a fantastic revelation of Himself in His Son and the written Word, committing Himself to us for now and eternity. Yet we still say that *if* God is with me, will do this for me, will guide me—a constant stream of "ifs"—we will serve him. Instead, we should be surrendering ourselves without reservation to the sovereign, omnipresent God.

What conditions have you set out before God to help you get out of your loneliness? Is He supposed to get you a roommate, a marriage partner, a more congenial office to work in? Surrender to Him in your loneliness, let Him be your all in all—and then see what He will do for you.

God taught Jacob that He was a trustworthy Father and an ever present companion, but also the ladder in Jacob's dream teaches us that *God is a loving Redeemer.* About fifteen hundred years after Jacob's experience, a man sat under a fig tree, meditating on the Scriptures. It seems he was reading the Old Testament, probably meditating on the story of Jacob and his dream (the clues are in what Jesus said to him later). Suddenly his reverie was broken by the arrival of Philip, who announced excitedly, "We have found Him of whom Moses in the Law and also the Prophets wrote" (John 1:45). Nathanael listened to Philip's whole story and then said somewhat disdainfully, "Can any good thing come out of Nazareth?" (John 1:46). Philip was not easily put off and said, in effect, "See for yourself."

When Nathanael and Philip came to Jesus, He said, "Behold, an Israelite indeed, in whom is no guile!" (John 1:47).

Nonplussed, Nathanael responded, "How do You know me?" (v. 48).

Jesus looked at him and said, "Before Philip called you, when you were under the fig tree, I saw you" (v. 48).

Nathanael was so overwhelmed that he blurted out, "Rabbi, You are the Son of God; You are the King of Israel" (v. 49). He had caught the clues that indicated

Jesus had seen him across the miles, meditating on Jacob, and had read what was in his mind. He did not need the later words of Jesus, "Truly, truly, I say to you, you shall see the heavens opened, and the angels of God ascending and descending upon the Son of Man" (v. 51), to recognize Jesus' references to Jacob's dream.

For us, however, that reference is significant, for you will notice that the angels are ascending and descending on the Son of Man, Jesus. The ladder thus becomes symbolic of God's blessings being brought to us through Jesus Christ. That is why the Bible says that God has blessed us with all spiritual blessings in heavenly places in Christ Jesus (Eph. 1:3). Our worship ascends to God as His blessings descend to us—and all of this is dependent upon the perfect merit of Jesus Christ.

Jesus Christ is the kinsman-Redeemer who puts, as it were, one hand on God the Father and the other one on man, bringing us together so that we can make contact with God the Father. Thus, today you can say that the ladder extends to any part of the world. Any room, any territory, no matter how isolated, can thus become the house of God and the gate of heaven.

We know, of course, that God created us as social beings—we need the companionship of others as well as the companionship of God. Many people simply do not take the initiative to make friends; they do not want to risk commitment to any relationship. Others, perhaps, have special barriers that prevent them from forming close friendships. If, for some reason, there is a void in your life; if you have lost a loved one or can't seem to form friendships; use this time of loneliness to become acquainted with God. Someone has said, "Loneliness is a signal that it's time for us to become better acquainted with God." That may sound simplistic, because God is invisible, but consider the words of Asaph: "Whom have I in heaven but Thee? And besides Thee, I desire nothing on earth" (Psalm 73:25). Don't dismiss the possibility that you might be on the verge of a giant step in your spiritual life. Read the Bible as a love letter; there can be something beautiful about a person left alone in the presence of Almighty God.

Where is God when you are lonely? Right beside you, willing to lift that blue feeling, give you purpose in life, Someone to live for. As Jacob did, you can experience the sure cure for loneliness as you worship in His presence where you are right now. A Father, companion, and Redeemer—that's what He wants to become in your life today.

Suggested Application

1. List all the reasons why it is possible to be lonely in a crowd.

2. What do we learn about God's provision for our companionship in Genesis 2:18? What provision ought the church to make for those who are presently unmarried?

3. Many people are lonely because they've been hurt. They do not want to risk further friendships. What can we do to help them overcome such fears?

4. Perhaps the most severe loneliness is that caused by rejection. Often, those who need friendship the most are rejected because of their personality, appearance, or lack of social graces. Specifically, what should we

do to give such people a sense of identity and a feeling that they belong?

5. To what extent can friendship with God meet our need for companionship? Consider Christ's repeated reference to His Father's presence (John 8:16-19).

8

Controlling Anger

MAVIS STEPPED up to her wall oven, switched on the light, and looked in. Tired after a hard day of cleaning, she had popped a nut loaf into the oven so her son would have a sweet for his lunch the next day. Now she watched as dough overflowed the loaf pan on every side and collected in little mounds on the bottom of a freshly cleaned oven.

Anger surged through her. She slammed her fist on the oven door. Expletives long buried in her subconscious exploded from her lips.

"Nothing I've done today has gone right!" she shouted. "Everything I do is a disaster. I can't even bake a simple loaf of bread without the dough running all over my clean oven. Look at it," she said angrily as her husband entered the room. "I got the recipe from my friend last week, and look at it on the floor of my oven."

She took the dish cloth and slammed it against the wall.

"You try to do something for someone, and look what happens."

Her husband retreated from the kitchen. He was glad that the children weren't in, or they might get caught in the barrage. He knew that Mavis's anger would soon be spent and she would be apologizing for it. Though this kind of scene had occurred frequently early in marriage, it was now a rarity and came only after many days of frustration in the office or at home. And a baking or cooking failure usually triggered it.

Mavis is like many of us. Most of the time we can control our anger. When resentments, frustration, hurt feelings, and simple fatigue accumulate, we explode. Is such anger always wrong, sometimes wrong—or maybe even sometimes right? Is there actually a time to get good and angry? Why did Paul remind us, "Be angry, and yet do not sin; do not let the sun go down on your anger, and do not give the devil an opportunity" (Eph. 4:26-27).

By now some of you are ready to tune me out or to read on only because you might be able to help a friend. You're saying, "I never get angry like that!" I'm not sure I should believe you—I am not convinced you are that dead! Maybe that's because I have a temper, an admission that may surprise some. More to the point is that God gets angry as well. We read in Psalm 7:11, "God is angry with the wicked every day" (KJV).

You say that is a different kind of anger. So did I, and I was convinced that God would have to reach down and change my emotional structure so I would never have those feelings of anger again. But I was wrong, and now I am glad God did not change my emotional makeup. When I realized that God becomes angry, I realized that anger as such is not sinful. Over and over again you read that God was angry with the people of Israel, that the anger of the Lord burned against them.

God's anger is not confined to the Old Testament, however. In Mark 3:5 we read that Jesus Christ went into the synagogue and "looked round about on them with anger" (KJV). Stop for a moment and imagine the scene. Jesus went into that synagogue on the Sabbath and noticed a man with a withered hand—probably planted there by the religious leaders to see what Jesus would do. Would He heal him on the Sabbath? Jesus, reading their minds, asked, "Is it lawful to do good on the sabbath days, or to do evil? to save life, or to kill?" (Mark 3:4, KJV). Their silence gave Him the answer, an answer that genuinely angered Him because it revealed the hardness of their hearts.

So we see that God the Father was angry, and God the Son became angry. Another Old Testament passage shows how the third Person in the Godhead can be involved. When the Ammonites surrounded the city of Jabesh-gilead and appeared strong enough to take the city, the city fathers volunteered to make a covenant with the Ammonites. They would become their servants. But Nahash, the Ammonite leader, demanded the right to put out the right eyes of the residents of the city before making peace. The elders of the city pleaded for time and sent out messengers to the rest of Israel, asking for help. When Saul heard this, "the Spirit of God came upon Saul . . . and he became very angry" (1 Sam. 11:6). That anger resulted in the deliverance of the people in the city of Jabesh-gilead.

Clearly, anger in itself is not sin; it is not evil. Anger is found within the Godhead; it is also part of being human. It is part of the emotional structure God built into us when He made us. He made us with the capacity for an emotional response, and we cannot and need not prevent those emotions from welling up.

As with so many areas of human experience, the Bible does provide a warning signal. Under the inspiration of the Holy Spirit, Paul wrote that we are not to sin when we get angry, indicating the very real possibility of sin when the emotional response of anger occurs.

The apostle Paul suggested that anger can be a real problem when he told the Ephesians, "Do not let the sun go down on your anger" (Eph. 4:26). Anger that persists beyond sundown is uncontrolled, and it is uncontrolled anger that causes our problems. It ruptures relationships, it stifles spiritual growth, it gives place to the devil (v. 27), and it opens the door to sinning.

Consider the carefully nourished relationship between a man and a woman during courtship and early marriage. There is good communication. One day a problem arises. The disagreement becomes so sharp that things get out of hand, and words are flung at each other like poison-tipped arrows. Later the husband can say that he is sorry, and the wife can say she is sorry. They forgive each other. At least they *say* they do. Yet both know something has happened to their relationship. There is something that cannot be regained because of the hurt. A relationship has experienced a rupture, and it may never grow together the way it once was.

Think of children growing up with deeply wounded spirits because of the unfairness of parents exercising discipline when extremely angry. It is not wrong to discipline children in anger, but it is wrong to discipline them when anger is out of control. Then the discipline becomes an emotional explosion instead of a corrective action growing out of love for the child. The resulting fracture in the parent-child relationship may widen during the rebellious teen years, and then concerned parents wonder, "What went wrong?"

Uncontrolled anger does not only affect others. It can stifle your spiritual growth because of a building sense of guilt and the resultant discouragement. I've known men who put a fist through the wall in a fit of anger. They then cried to the Lord in their feelings of guilt, asking for deliverance. They wanted deliverance because they wanted to be spared the embarrassment of doing something foolish.

Many times such explosions of anger are merely a symptom of unresolved problems. The explosion is like the tip of the iceberg, revealing only a little of the submerged anger. Such people may be angry at life itself, or they may be angry at their marriage partner, their children, or God Himself. At the least provocation, their anger flames up uncontrolled. The sense of guilt felt by such people only fuels the anger.

Under such conditions, it is not surprising that uncontrolled anger gives place to the devil. That is clearly what Paul implied when he wrote in Ephesians 4:27 that we are not to give place to the devil. Uncontrolled anger gives place to the devil because of the thoughts revealed by the torrent of words in such moments—and often by our irrational behavior. In Mavis's case, the words used when the dough ran over the top of the baking pan were clearly not under the control of the Holy Spirit, but came from a time when Satan ruled her life.

With that experience as a wedge, the devil then whispers words of discouragement, of hopelessness. All the other weapons in his arsenal are quickly marshaled, and unless the Christian recognizes what is going on and seeks forgiveness from the Lord and others involved, Satan will have a field day. No wonder the Scriptures indicate that anger is closely related to demonic activity.

Hard to believe? Not really, when you see people throwing things in anger, putting their feet or fists through walls. I've known people who attempted to track down the root of such anger and discovered it started after they dabbled in some occult practice and attended seances.

The potential for sinning is revealed when we examine the way people handle anger. Some people admit, "I just blow up." Others express it less dramatically: "I just give him a piece of my mind." Actually, most of us cannot afford to do that—that's why we read in the book of Proverbs that the discreet person is slow to anger (Prov. 16:32). Some people tell us we will "feel better" when we blow up, but in the process we say and do things better left unsaid and undone.

Nor can I recommend handling anger the way some psychologists suggest. They say we should take a pillow and pretend that the pillow is the object of our anger: our mother, wife, husband, child, or employer. Then really pound the pillow until you feel better. Unfortunately, that merely fuels our anger and provides no permanent release. It certainly is not the biblical way of handling anger.

A less destructive way of handling anger is to clam up. Such people know the explosion will result in ruptured relationships, so they say, "I'd rather not say anything." Instead they seethe, like Mount St. Helens in Washington. They may or may not blow up occasionally. Even if they don't, their failure to communicate also damages relationships. Clamming up is definitely not a biblical way of handling anger, for it is a refusal to face the issues that God wants a person to face. This stunts growth in relationships, does not resolve tensions, and will probably result in physical symptoms that seem unexplainable.

The Bible provides a beautiful example, in the life of Nehemiah, of how to control anger. Nehemiah had come back to Jerusalem from a fine position in the court of Artaxerxes to supervise the rebuilding of the walls of Jerusalem. A delegation of Hebrews had come with him, and I suspect some had come because of the opportunities to make an extra shekel during such a period of progress. These and local opportunists had used a period of scarcity to claim both fields and daughters from those who owed them money.

We read in Nehemiah 5 that when he became aware of what was going on, "I was very angry when I had heard their outcry" (v. 6). Now that's the kind of anger I appreciate and would encourage. I wish that we had people today who could get angry at the sort of shows seen on television, at the violence and child abuse in homes. I would like to see more people become angry at the child neglect in our country, at the social injustice, at racial discrimination—and begin to do some things about them. Jesus did when He rid the Temple of those who were defiling it by fleecing the people and getting rich on dishonest gain.

Nehemiah's anger resulted in positive action. Notice the steps. First, *he admitted he was angry.* He wrote it down for all of us to become aware of it. Praise God for someone who can admit to being angry!

A preacher friend tells of the time in a deacon's meeting when one of the men pounded his fist on the table and glared at those around it in obvious anger. When admonished he said, "What do you mean? I'm not angry." He refused to admit his anger. He's like the person who says that he's forgiven so-and-so and then hands you a list of the offenses forgiven. The list might as well have been written in concrete.

Nehemiah could have said, "I'll let sleeping dogs lie." But if he had done that, the whole place would have been filled with sleeping dogs! Instead he said, "I was very angry," and in the following verses we see how he could be both good and angry.

In verse 7, the Bible reveals that *he consulted with himself.* He thought it through before he used his tongue.

He did not say the first thing that popped into his head. He did not let Satan drive a wedge in his relationship with the people by saying the first thing he thought of.

Consider how this applies in a marriage relationship. Many times a legitimate issue is being discussed at the wrong time. A man works hard to earn the money to provide for his family. The wife works hard to keep the house, prepare the food, and look after the children. All day long, he's been thinking about the race car he and his friends are building. He promises himself that as soon as supper is over, he'll get with his friends and forget the boredom of his job. He comes home, gives his wife a quick peck on the cheek, makes sure Johnny gets away from the television and to the supper table, eats his meal, and heads for the door.

About this time, the pent-up frustration of the weary wife surfaces.

"There you go again. You're so selfish. You never think of anyone but yourself!"

Suddenly the husband feels guilty about what he had looked forward to all day. Yet he has promised his friends, and not to go would mean disappointing them and losing face. He slams the door and heads for his car.

Understand, the wife is probably right. But that is the wrong time to throw that accusation at him. At that moment, the wife needs to "consult" with herself and ask the Lord for wisdom to bring up the issue at the right time, for there is clearly a problem.

"Hey," you say, "I am one of those who gets so overwhelmed by my emotions that there is no way under the sun I will be able to control my anger in a situation like that." Really? I am sure you remember a time when you were in the middle of a heated argument and the telephone rang. You walked over to the phone and said

"Hello" in the friendliest of voices. After the conversation, your argument continued where it left off.

Why were you able to be so calm on the phone?
Obviously, you wanted to impress your friend and
didn't want him to know you were in the middle of a fit
of anger. The same is true when you get angry at your
boss.

I remember a professor at the university who really
upset me. I could cheerfully have told him off in no
uncertain terms, but I did not. And I am glad I did not,
for it would have ruptured a relationship, and in many
ways I respect him highly.

Amazingly, we seem to hurt most those who are
closest to us. We have so much respect for our boss that
we won't tell him off. Yet we explode at our wife or
husband, the person we promised to love and cherish.

James gives us a comparison between the tongue and
a little rudder that can steer a large ship. Yes, a small
rudder can control a large ship; so the tongue controls
the whole body. According to James, if we do not
"stumble" in what we say, we are able to bridle the
whole body as well. That's a man of discipline! Yet
James also makes it clear that "no one can tame the
tongue" by himself (3:8). That is why the Bible lists
self-control as part of the fruit of the Spirit (Gal. 5:23).

Nehemiah "consulted with himself" to gain control of
his thoughts before he expressed his anger. I have
found that a simple thing like counting to twenty can
help tremendously in putting my thoughts into low
gear and helping to control my tongue. If Mavis had
done that, her reaction would have been much less vio-
lent.

Once Nehemiah had his thoughts in order, he "con-
tended with the nobles" (5:7). He recognized that something had to be done, that he could not stand idly by

while widows and children were enslaved and the property of the sick was seized by mortgage holders. So, *he communicated his carefully considered proposal,* insisting on action.

Your husband never puts his dirty shirt in the laundry basket? You can kick it, slam it into the basket, even tear it up in anger, but that will not change his habit. Notice that in Ephesians 4, the verse preceding the admonition on anger charges us to speak the truth, while the verse after the challenge to "let all bitterness and wrath and anger . . . be put away from you" (Eph. 4:31) reminds us to "be kind to one another, tenderhearted" (v. 32). So instead of kicking the shirt every time it lies on the floor, talk to him about it at a time when you can do it kindly and dispassionately. Then if he should remind you of a habit that upsets him, you can also accept it without anger.

Nehemiah knew that if he kept quiet and stewed about it, a great deal of tension could build up. At the earliest opportunity he confronted the leadership and suggested a plan of action. No doubt it was tougher to do that than keep quiet, but the longer he waited the harder it would get.

The devil has a way of helping us postpone positive, stress-reducing communication. Or he likes to see us skirt the issue, beat around the bush. Maybe we mention it in prayer meeting, asking others to pray about it, rather than move into a loving, biblical confrontation.

Or we simply avoid the topics that could provide disagreement. Maybe at this moment you are saying, "That's us. We never discuss discipline of children" or "We never discuss my mother-in-law." Instead of resolving differences in loving communication, we let our bodies absorb the effects of that tension—and our children experience confusion because we as parents are not agreed on when and how to administer discipline; nor are they sure how to respond to the relatives.

When Nehemiah moved to communicate his reaction to what he saw, he prepared a solution to the problem. In verse 11 of chapter 5 he said, "Please, give back to them this very day"—and then he listed what needed to be restored. And it was done! Would that have happened if he had simply berated them in his anger?

Most solutions you and I propose will not get the response Nehemiah received: "Then the people did according to his promise" (5:13). A compromise will be a more likely result. The husband working on the racing car with his friends may agree to a less frequent schedule and also to a larger involvement in the home. In return for watching a particular football game, the husband may agree to take his wife out to dinner at her favorite restaurant. *Whatever the compromise, the proposing of creative solutions is a far more effective release of energy than blowing up or clamming up.*

You are married to one of those uncommunicative types, or you work for one at the office or factory? There may well be many times when the only thing you can do is to spend a lot of time communicating with God, asking for wisdom on how to unlock a life that does not want to communicate. You cannot simply give up, for if the person you are living with does not want to communicate, there are clearly unresolved conflicts he is not able to face. Guilt freezes the lines of communication.

Forgiveness may be the necessary alternative. In your anger, you may have been showing an unforgiving spirit that is blocking communication. The Bible is very clear that we are to forgive one another unconditionally, no matter how seriously we have been offended or hurt.

Sometimes repentance is the only solution. A father of five in Detroit went golfing early Saturday morning and then went to the church where a revival meeting was in progress. Of the two hundred men attending the meeting, half were on their knees before God. When he saw the men weeping before God, he pounded his fist into his hand and said, "You'll never get me, God."

Why did he say that? Because he had a hot temper and five children, an unfortunate combination. Through the years he had deeply wounded the spirits of those children, and he knew that if God ever got hold of him, he would have to repent and ask forgiveness of his children. Eventually, God "got" him. When he sought the forgiveness of his children, the experience was used by the Lord to soften the hearts of the whole family.

Dealing with our anger may thus involve compromise, it may mean forgiving others who have wounded us and do not ask for forgiveness, and it may necessitate repentance. Only when this happens can the anger within us be resolved so it does not stay inside us forever.

Nehemiah represents the person who was good and angry. He was angry at sin and injustice, at the suffering of the poor at the hands of the greedy. He also represents the person who channels his anger creatively for positive results. He controlled his tongue until he had thought it through. Then he communicated in a positive manner what was in his heart. Finally, he proposed a solution that, although in many ways unpalatable, could be implemented.

God does not want us to live with uncontrolled anger. He even sets a deadline—let not the sun go down on your wrath. Only then will we avoid giving the devil an opportunity to lead us to sin. Then we will have the inner release that contributes to healthy spirit, mind, and body. Ultimately that release is honoring to God, for it lets others know that the Holy Spirit is in charge of our lives.

Suggested Application

If you have an uncontrollable temper, here are some specific instructions that will enable you to exercise control:

1. Choose to forgive those who have wronged you. Lay down all bitterness (Eph. 4).

2. Begin each day by resisting Satan, especially that spirit of anger, and focus your mind on the promises of God. (This must be done *before* you encounter those stressful situations during the day.)

3. Accept your circumstances as from God. Your employer or partner is being used by God to develop the fruit of the Spirit in your life. Thank God for those difficult moments when you can prove His power.

4. Ask God to release the power of the Holy Spirit within you. Part of the fruit of the Spirit is "self-control."

5. If you do lose control, confess your sin to God and the person who was the object of your derision. Do this immediately.

6. Pray that God will give you wisdom to (a) become aware of a solution for the point of tension that causes the anger and (b) communicate your feelings to the person involved in the right *way* and at the

right *time*. Remember that your struggle is God's means of growth in your life.

9

Overcoming Disappointment

WHEN I joined the faculty of the Moody Bible Institute some years ago, the secretary for our section of faculty offices was a friendly, bright-eyed, twenty-year-old woman whose cheerful smile greeted everyone who walked past her desk. Three months later, a massive tumor was found in her abdomen. The doctors concluded she had only three months to live.

Debbie left for a hospital that specialized in cancer treatment. When she came back, the cancer was in remission and it seemed as though she was cured. You can imagine the tremendous feelings of relief and joy in the family and among her new friends at Moody. But the cancer did start to grow again, and Debbie died some months later.

Can you visualize what it must have been like to be lifted to the heavens, as it were, with those great feelings of joy and anticipation for a new lease on life, only to have all hope dashed to the ground? During that time, Debbie no doubt had to fight a tremendous sense of disappointment, as did her family and friends. The temporary promise of healing only heightened the disappointment.

Yet people like Debbie are not the only ones experiencing deep feelings of disappointment. You take a new job in a new community, hoping to find a more congenial work environment, only to find that office politics are just as rampant as at the job you left. Your superior is promoted, and you know you can handle the job—but someone else gets it. He's fifteen years younger than you are and not half as experienced.

As a parent, you may be disappointed in your children's actions. A woman who had once been a Bible class teacher said, "Long ago I've given up on God and on prayer. For nineteen years I prayed that my daughter would grow up to be a missionary. Not only has she not become a missionary, but she is now married to an unsaved man." Looking wistfully into the distance, she said, "I don't want to ask God for anything else because I don't want to be hurt and disappointed again."

Disappointment. It strikes all of us at one time or another. If these feelings are fed, they grow until they strangle our spiritual lives.

The Bible tells us about a time of severe disappointment experienced by the Children of Israel (Exod. 15:22-27). The Israelites had just come through the Red Sea, which the Lord had gloriously opened up for them. The first part of chapter 15 records their response to what God had done in a song so full of ecstatic praise that you are sure they will trust the Lord even in the most difficult of situations. (Eons later, another triumphant group will also sing "the song of Moses," as described in Revelation 15:3. These will also have "come off victorious from the beast and from his image and from the number of his name, standing on the sea of glass, holding harps of God" [Rev. 15:2]. Their song will be: "Great and marvelous are Thy works, O Lord God, the Almighty" [Rev. 15:3].)

But the heights of ecstasy did not last long in Moses' day! Tramping across the hot desert sand quickly reduced their supply of water to a sip now and then. For three days they looked for water and found none. Repeatedly the scouts came back with negative reports. It is clear from the tone of the narrative that anxiety was increasing.

Let me assure you before continuing that this is not just a story of the Israelites. It is our story as well. To recognize that, we must understand their circumstances better.

Some years ago it was my privilege to travel to Mount Sinai. We spent two days in a bus going from Jerusalem to Mount Sinai, and two days in our return. I vividly remember those buses getting stuck in the sand. We had to get out and push our bus just as though we were stuck in a snow bank. I remember how thirsty we became. We determined, however, not to drink any water except what we had brought along, fearing we would get ill if we drank any other. But when our water ran out, we drank whatever water was available.

"But surely Israel could have trusted God," you say. Yet for the Children of Israel in the desert, God seemed to be as elusive as the water they were looking for. Remember, this was at the start of forty years of maturing in the faith, and they had a long way to grow before they could be called strong in the faith.

Then came the word, "We have found an oasis. There's water just ahead." Parents encouraged their children, saying, "Just one more mile and we'll be there." Yet when they arrived, they discovered water so bitter they could not drink it.

"They were not thirsty enough," you say. Not true, for there are places where the water is so bitter that you cannot swallow it even if you are burning with thirst.

Then the grumbling set in. They had experienced a tremendous feeling of exhilaration as they approached the oasis, convinced that they would be able to slake their thirst. This made the disappointment so much greater—how could God play games with them? He led them to an oasis and their hopes soared, only to be dashed to the ground.

I believe we can learn something about overcoming disappointment from this experience of the Children of Israel. To draw out the truths, we will ask several questions. First, What causes disappointment? What caused this extreme disillusionment among the Israelites?

The answer, as I see it, is a wrong focus. You see, the Children of Israel had their minds and hearts set on two things. The first was the circumstance, the desire for water. I am not blaming them, for I am quite sure I would have been looking at the same thing. Yet the Israelites had their hearts so set on water, and on drinking it, that when the seemingly improved circumstance proved unsatisfactory, they blamed Moses and God.

They did not remember, as we don't most of the time, that when our hearts are set on something in this world, we stand a good chance of bitter disappointment. You have set your heart, for example, on getting a promotion. As far as you are concerned, it is "in the bag." Done. You have worked hard for it and you deserve it. When it is given to another, the bottom drops out of your world.

Or maybe you had your heart set on marriage. You meet another person with the same desire. You sense that it will work. Yet soon after the wedding, you realize he's not the kind of husband you expected. As the years pass, the differences grow, as does the strain in the marriage relationship. Initially the disappointment is mingled with the hope that things will get better. As the days roll into months and years, there is less hope and more disappointment. Why did God let this happen to you?

In both instances, as in Israel, the focus was on the circumstances, not on God. You were hoping circumstances would bring you joy, forgetting that joy comes only out of your relationship with Jesus Christ. As long as our hope is based on some thing or a combination of circumstances in this world, the risk of disappointment is great.

Second, the Children of Israel had their hopes pinned on a person, Moses. After all, he had been involved in such an astonishing number of miracles. So when the water was bitter, they grumbled to Moses, "So what's this? You take us into the desert three days and lead us to an oasis with bitter water. What kind of leadership is that?"

You know, of course, that they were not really grumbling against Moses. Their complaint was with God. Every complaint against the circumstances of life, unless they can be changed by us, is in reality a complaint against God. When it is cold and the snow is piled ten feet high, we complain about it. Then when summer comes and the heat and humidity wilt collars and raise tempers, we complain again. Since we cannot change the weather, you know who's responsible for it!

I mentioned expectations on entering marriage. On a list of ten reasons why marriages fail, unrealistic expectations is at the top. People expect a partner to provide what only God can do for them. One woman wrote that she had made her "Prince Charming" the king in her life. When he left her after twenty years of marriage, she was no longer the queen, and it devastated her. She made little progress, despite several stays in a mental hospital, until a friend invited her to a Bible study.

There she found that Jesus could meet her heart's need in a way her husband had never been able to.

You say, "I am happily married and that would never happen to me." But any human being is a potential broken reed. Only Jesus will never disappoint you. For that reason alone, your focus even in a happy marriage needs to be on your relationship to God.

One of the most widespread causes for disappointment is the discovery that a spiritual leader has feet of clay. We can put up with bad breath, with his not always remembering names. But when he loses his temper, when he is rude to a waitress, or if he fails morally, we can be shaken in our faith in God because the disappointment is so great. Unfortunately, we have superstars in Christianity just as the world has its superstars. We forget that Jesus alone is the "superstar" in Christianity. The psalmist had come to terms with that when he wrote, "My soul, wait in silence for God only, for my hope is from Him" (Psalm 62:5). That's an important lesson to learn if we want to overcome life's disappointments.

Have you ever thought of the fact that our disappointments are God's way of reminding us that there are idols in our lives that must be dealt with? In Psalm 73, the psalmist Asaph told us that he looked at the rich and noticed that they were often wicked people. He wondered why he did not have wealth like that as a servant of God. You remember that he admitted, "My steps had almost slipped. For I was envious of the arrogant, as I saw the prosperity of the wicked" (Psalm 73:2-3). Then one day he went into the Temple and God reminded him of the end of the wicked. He quickly realized that the rich were indeed in deep trouble and that his riches were in reality far greater than theirs. That's why he could say, "Whom have I in heaven but

Thee? And beside Thee, I desire nothing on earth" (v. 25). In effect he said, "God, You are my all." It is only when you discover that you have nothing left but God that you realize God is enough.

The Children of Israel arrived at Marah, their hearts set on improved circumstances, on an abundance of sweet water, on another great display of leadership by Moses, and they were severely disappointed. They had not yet learned that God wants us to recognize that He alone is the one who can fully meet our expectations.

I remember how I had to learn this lesson. I was extremely elated because of the response to something I had written by someone I greatly admired. As I was rejoicing, the Holy Spirit put a damper on my joy, reminding me that some things I would do would be severely criticized. If my heart was set on getting the praise of men, I would sooner or later be disappointed, but if I looked for God's approval, He would not disappoint me.

Our second question is, What is the remedy for disappointment? Fortunately, the story in Exodus 15 does not stop with the disappointment. Moses had listened to the grumbling of the people. You can take only so much of that, so he shut them out and started talking to God. In fact, the Bible uses a much stronger word than that: he cried out to the Lord. The Lord responded by showing him a tree that he cut down and threw into the water. Whether the tree was known for its ability to turn bitter water into sweet drinking water does not matter. The fact is that he saw the tree only when he called upon the Lord.

When Hurricane Allen hit the coast of Texas, it carried a tidal wave in front of it. Right about now you may feel as though you have been hit by that tidal wave, your disappointment is so great. All you can think about is unrealized expectations. Yet now is the time to remember what Moses did—he cried out to the Lord.

Prayer is that mighty power that is swifter than an eagle, stronger than a lion. Prayer puts you in touch with the resources of a compassionate and holy God. And when Moses prayed, a miracle started unfolding. He saw a tree that turned their situation totally around, that alleviated their disappointment.

Even if the tree had the ability to turn bitter water into sweet water, there's no way it could have been effective for all the water on the oasis. God did a miracle, changing the bitter water into the sweetest drinking water Israel had ever known. That's one way God responds to our disappointments. He changes the circumstances in response to prayer.

There are times when life's disappointments become God's opportunity to do a miracle. The person who was promoted ahead of you is hired away by another company, and this time you get promoted. Your marriage partner goes off to a retreat, meets the Lord in a vital way, and begins fulfilling your expectations. Your child joins a canoeing expedition and there in the wilderness recognizes the rotten way he's been treating you.

Remember when Jesus calmed the sea with but a word? Remember how the storm stopped when Jesus got into the boat after He came walking to the disciples on the water? He changed the water into wine, raised Jairus's daughter and the son of the widow of Nain, and fed five thousand with five loaves and two fish. He can do it today.

I believe, however, that God wants to do an even greater miracle than turning our bitter circumstances into something sweet. Suppose you have a very responsible position in your community. You are determined that nothing, no one, not even your children, is going to damage your reputation. Then your son goes to a party where there are alcoholic beverages, and he partakes of them. On the way home, he loses control of his car and it crashes into a tree. The girl with him is killed, and your son walks away almost unscathed. Not surprisingly, you and your wife are very angry, bitter about a home that served alcohol, and resentful that your son is now the talk of the town.

What would be the greatest miracle in relation to your disappointment? Would it not be taking away the resentment and bitterness, the anger and extreme disappointment, replacing it with the grace and ability to accept that son even though he disappointed you? God can do it and is doing it in families today.

God can begin to make you accept that person your daughter married. He can give you inner release from the anger generated when your husband is trapped by his desires on a business trip. The circumstances may remain unchanged, but God can help you to discover His sweetness in the midst of bitter water.

Furthermore, many people believe that the tree Moses threw into the bitter water was symbolic of the cross. You'll remember that Eve ate from the forbidden tree and then gave the fruit to Adam, who also ate. That tree poisoned all the waters of humanity from that time on. The gospels draw our attention to another tree, the cross on which Jesus Christ died, absorbing all the hurts and disappointments, all the consequences of sin, for all humanity. He thereby made a payment for sin so that man could be in touch with God again, providing a way through which the bitterness of life could become sweet. Even death, that most bitter of experiences, can be sweetened because of the cross.

The apostle Paul reminded us of the significance of the cross in Galatians 6:14. Though he had had many bitter disappointments in life, he wrote, "But may it never be that I should boast, except in the cross of our Lord Jesus Christ." *He knew that if you begin to glory in something other than the cross, you are headed for disappointment.* It may be at the beginning of life, in the middle of life, or at the end, but it will come.

Notice Paul's conclusion: "through which the world has been crucified to me, and I to the world" (6:14). He was saying that the way God takes care of disappointment in life is to wean us from all the world's things, to wean us from the secret pleasures, to make us dead to all those impulses that seem to give us such pleasure in life. As we through the Holy Spirit come alive to God, He can somehow sweeten the harsh and bitter experiences.

That does not mean we become immune to all the disappointments of life. Disappointments will come because we remain human, but it does mean that those bitter waters of disappointment can be made sweet through the forgiveness of Christ and the acceptance we receive in Christ through the power of the cross.

Think of that disappointment that is eating away at you right now. Bring it to the cross, receive forgiveness for your lack of faith and trust in God, and expose it to His ability to heal.

Let me ask a final question. What is the challenge of disappointment? As I see it, the challenge is to obedience. Notice what it says in Exodus 15:25-26: "There He made for them a statute and regulation, and there He tested them. And He said, 'If you will give earnest heed to the voice of the LORD your God, and do what is right in His eyes, and give ear to His commandments, and keep all His statutes, I will put none of the diseases on you which I have put on the Egyptians; for I, the LORD, am your healer.' "

According to the biblical record, the experience at Marah was a test, establishing a pattern that God followed throughout the Old Testament. God *tested* the Children of Israel to see what was in their heart, to see if they would really keep His commandments.

Focus on that disappointment in your life. Think of it in terms of a test permitted by God to see if you will obey Him, trust Him, believe that He desires the best for you. Or are you going to say, "OK, God, it's all over. I'm through. I'm finished with You. You did not take care of this circumstance as I expected You would. You didn't answer my prayer. You didn't do what *I knew* You ought to do, so I'm through."

If you think of every disappointment as a test, it becomes an opportunity to say, "God, I'm going to readjust my focus. I'm going to learn my lesson. I'm going to trust You to do that miracle in my heart."

After the test of obedience, the Children of Israel experienced God's reward. He had told them that if they responded properly, He would not afflict them with all the diseases He had put on the Egyptians during the plagues. In effect, the Lord said, "I will be in the midst of your circumstances. I will protect you from some of the harsh realities of existence. I will bring you all the way into the land because I will physically give you the strength, and I will protect you from disease."

Immediately after this commitment on God's part, the people arrived at Elim, where there were twelve springs, one for every tribe in Israel. Seventy date palms dotted the skyline to relieve the monotony of the desert, and it may be that they also provided a change in diet. Supplied with all the water they needed, the Children Of Israel settled down for a refreshing interlude.

Have you ever noticed that disappointments give life

a roller-coaster effect? You go through extremely disappointing times, not realizing there is an Elim ahead.
Even the tall palms are not yet visible. Yet God has a
reward waiting when you pass the test of obedience,
something extra-special if you obey the voice of the
Lord.

Several years ago I met a young man in Denver who
is very good at speculating on where oil wells might be.
Not surprisingly, he has become very wealthy. One
time he made a bid on a contract that was very important to him. Because of a technicality, he missed getting
the contract. He told me that when he came home, he
felt so disappointed that he became physically sick. In
telling me about it he said, "As a result of that experience, I made a vow to God that I would never again set
my heart on anything in this world other than my relationship to the Lord God." That young man responded
correctly to the test of obedience. Subsequently, he was
awarded contracts many times larger than the one he
failed to win.

As I move about, I meet many who have had bitterly
disappointing experiences. I discover that a variety of
"trees" has been offered to them. You may even have
tried to sweeten the bitter water in your life with one of
them.

One of the trees highly recommended to remove bitterness is riches. People think that if they could only
become rich, all the bitterness would disappear. Yet
there is ample evidence in the personal testimony of
rich people that riches are no cure for disappointment.
In fact, they turn bitter water into poison.

Another highly recommended tree is the tree of pleasure. It grows with sturdy and deep roots. It promises
to remove the monotony of existence and replace it with
excitement and glitter. Just nibble at it, people say, and

you'll find it a lot easier to make it from weekend to weekend. Yet even though man has more time for pleasure and a greater variety of ways to experience it, we see unhappiness everywhere. The divorce rate is just one indication that people are not happier.

For years, drugs and alcohol were touted as the great escape from disappointment. But the increasing rate of suicide among people who use drugs and alcohol clearly shows that this tree cannot sweeten the bitter waters.

The greatest disappointments in life come from unfulfilled expectations, unrealized dreams, and the only "tree" that will sweeten the bitter waters of disappointment is the Lord Himself. The apostle Paul came to realize this after he met Christ. He wrote to the Philippians, "I count all things to be loss in view of the surpassing value of knowing Christ Jesus my Lord, for whom I have suffered the loss of all things, and count them but rubbish in order that I may gain Christ" (3:8). Only when your expectations are focused on Christ can you overcome the disappointments of life. He is an expert at healing the brokenhearted. Thus, your *disappointment* can become God's *appointment* to discover that He alone must be your pleasure, your desire, the focus of your heart's affection.

Suggested Application

1. Study Luke 24:1-35 as an example of the cause and cure for disappointment. Answer these questions:

   - Since the disciples' conception of the Messiah was quite accurate (vv. 19-21), what specifically caused them to be so disappointed in Him?

- • What very important bits of information were the disciples missing in their conception of what they expected Christ to do or not to do?

- • To what did Christ point them in their disappointment, and how should it have helped them?

- • These disciples eventually returned to Jerusalem with courage and joy. What made the difference? How should this apply to us today?

2. Give examples of disappointment in your own life. Were your hopes pinned on some circumstance or human goal? What lesson, if any, did you learn from the experience?

10

Moving from Regret to Restoration

"FOR OF all the sad words of tongue and pen, the saddest are these, 'It might have been.' " So wrote John Greenleaf Whittier.

I think all of us can identify with that statement. All of us have suffered from feelings of regret. We know the pain and agony regret brings into our lives. We keep thinking how really different it all could have been if—if—if. You complete the sentence.

There are at least two kinds of regret. There is the regret caused by making human error. You make an honest mistake, but it may have had disastrous consequences, and you have to live with them.

I read of an incident involving a missionary airplane mechanic. He had serviced airplanes for years and had an excellent record. One day he had just completed the initial hand-tightening on a nut when he was called away. Completely distracted by the new problem, he forgot to tighten the nut with a wrench.

The airplane took off with seven people in it. Because that nut was not adequately tightened, gasoline started leaking out. The plane eventually caught fire and crashed, killing all seven aboard.

That mechanic attended the funeral and saw the seven coffins lined up in a row. Waves of regret washed over him in his agony of soul and spirit. One momentary lapse and seven lives had been snuffed out. Children lost their fathers, and there were several mothers newly widowed.

You may have been driving carefully in a residential district. The curb was lined with cars. You were distracted by a person on one side of the street for a moment. As your eyes refocused on the road ahead of you, you saw a toddler run into the street. You slammed on the brakes, but it was too late. Even though you were not really responsible for the death of the child, you experience tremendous feelings of regret.

In such cases, we must ask others to forgive us for our errors in judgment. The missionary mechanic was fortunate because he was assured by the bereaved that they understood that everyone makes errors. They were not angry at him. It took months, but eventually the mechanic overcame his despondency and fierce regret. Receiving the forgiveness of others enabled him to forgive himself.

Although such feelings of regret are difficult to live with, they are not brought on by the Holy Spirit. They result from human error, which we are all subject to daily. Obviously, some of us are more prone to such error because of lack of education, experience, or physical limitations. It is not God's intention, however, that we get bogged down by our inability to forgive ourselves. God judges us by our intentions, not according to our human frailty.

There's a second form of regret that grows out of deliberate disobedience. We choose a certain lifestyle even though we know it is wrong. A small voice in us tells us our choice is sinful, but we continue that lifestyle anyway. One day we look in the family album and see what we looked like as a little boy or little girl, and we suddenly wonder what life would have been like if our choices had been different.

Or the regret may come at the end of life as death approaches. A friend went to see a former employer, a newspaper publisher, in the hospital. When the publisher saw my friend, he asked that the door be closed. Then he asked that my friend read the Bible for him and pray with him.

"I know I am going to die. I have wasted my life in a vain pursuit of riches and public acclaim. Now I realize my mistake and want to get right with God," the publisher said.

Sometimes a father experiences a similar regret when his children have all left home. He wishes he had taken more time with them—he hardly knows them now. The regret will not change what has happened in the past, but it can lead to future changes. God can still use that emotion of regret to make the best of the future.

So what can you do about regret? What response will minimize the agony of regret and help you cope with the memory of missed opportunities or wrong decisions? The Bible provides an example that can be most helpful to you and me.

The initial incident is found in Luke 22:31-34. Read it carefully, for it sets the stage for a decision that Peter, the disciple of Christ, will deeply regret.

Peter is at the final meal with Jesus. They have just had what we now call the Lord's Supper. Then the disciples got into a major argument over who was the greatest among them, a development Jesus used to teach them about servant leadership roles. I sense that Peter must have been a central figure in the argument, for Jesus turned to him by name and warned him that Satan desired to sift him like wheat. Then Jesus said something that came back to haunt Peter: "I have prayed for you, that your faith may not fail; and you, when you have turned again, strengthen your brothers" (v. 32). The implication in that sentence is that Peter would fail and be restored.

Peter did not like that implication. He had all the credentials for being a winning member of the team, so he determined to reassure Jesus. He proudly asserted, "Lord, with You I am ready to go both to prison and to death" (v. 33).

Have you ever prayed and as you did thought, *God ought to be really impressed with the promise I am making. At least He can depend on me.* As you thought that, you had forgotten that you can keep no promises made to God except the ones made in total dependence upon Him, recognizing the need for His grace to live as you should.

Weeks and months later, Peter may have been saying to himself, "Me and my big mouth. I'm constantly getting in deeper than I can handle. If only I didn't need to show off my commitment so much." You see, the bigger the promise, the harder the fall.

You know the rest of the story. Peter obviously boasted too much, prayed too little, acted too soon, and almost got himself arrested for cutting off a guard's ear. Later he followed too far off, considered what he was saying too little, and generally ended up digging a real grave for himself. The crow of a rooster and a glance from Jesus brought him down to earth. Mark, the gospel writer, reported the result: "And he began to weep" (Mark 14:72).

Why did he weep bitterly? I think it was because he was in the very presence of Jesus when he denied Him. Jesus was within the line of his vision when the servant girl came and said to him, "You, too, were with Jesus the Nazarene" (Mark 14:67). Overcome by fear of the results if he admitted allegiance to his Master, he denied that he had ever known Jesus (Mark 14:68).

Those kinds of denials are hard to understand and accept. Peter had been with Jesus three years. He had shared the platform with Him at many a large gathering. Jesus had healed his mother-in-law. And Peter had made that soul-stirring affirmation, "Thou art the Christ, the Son of the living God" (Matt. 16:16). Now the accusative tone in a girl's voice brought from Peter's lips an abject denial. In fact, I suspect Peter later had trouble accepting the fact that he had really done it. He couldn't believe his own memory. That's regret.

In spite of all that, Peter's experience provides us with clear guidelines on how to move from regret to restoration, how you can move from bitterness over some experience in your past to blessing. Through the experience of Peter, God draws back the curtain a bit and lets us gain at least some understanding of what is going on in the great drama of life. It shows how you who are living in the far country of regret can be restored to meaningful fellowship with the Savior.

The first truth to accept is that *Jesus Christ prays for you*. When you examine Luke 22:31, you will notice that Jesus addressed Peter as "Simon," using the name that refers to his humanity. At that moment he was not Peter, the rock, but Simon, the human being, open to the temptation of Satan.

There is an interesting contrast in the Greek New Testament. When Jesus said, "Satan has demanded permission to sift you," the word *you* is plural. Christ was apparently speaking to all the disciples. But when He continued, "but I have prayed for you," the word *you* is singular. Now the focus is directly on Peter, that his faith fail not.

Why did Jesus pray for Peter? Was it because Peter held such a lofty position in the group? Hardly. Peter was the rash and egotistical one. He was not the mild-mannered, consistent follower.

"Aha," you say. "I know why Jesus prayed for Peter. It was because Peter was the bold, strong one, the man who was able to make wise decisions for the group."

Wrong again. The reason Jesus prayed for Peter was precisely that he was so weak, that he was the kind of person who can be tripped up easily. You show me a man who is wretched, who is broken up emotionally, who cries out to God in the agony of his soul; you show me a woman who is fallen and crushed by her sin, who is unstable and unable to get a grip on her emotions; and I will show you a person upon whom the grace and mercy of Jesus Christ rest.

You remember the story of the shepherd. He had ninety-nine fine, obedient sheep in the fold. Yet there was one that had gone astray, who was outside in the night, and that is the one who got the attention of the shepherd. In the same way, Jesus sees everyone reading this page, but He is looking particularly at the one who is following afar off, whose faith has almost failed, who has denied the Lord and seems to be outside the embrace of God. He has prayed for you in a personal way, as He prayed especially for Peter so that he would not be totally overwhelmed by regret.

Significantly, Jesus' prayer is not a "bless everyone" generalization. It has a focus, Satan and his activity in the life of Peter. Jesus said, "Simon, Simon, behold, Satan has demanded permission to sift you like wheat; but I have prayed for you, that your faith may not fail."

When wheat grows, it has a protective coating called chaff around the grain. In the old-fashioned winnowing of Jesus' day, the chaff was separated from the wheat by throwing the mixture into the air while the wind was blowing. Modern harvesting equipment uses a sieve.

Jesus was saying to Peter, "Satan wants to sift you and prove that you are nothing but chaff."

You ask, "Does my exposure to temptation really have anything to do with evil spirits? Does it have anything to do with Satan?" Yes, it does. Peter did not see it that way, nor do many today. But the Lord draws the curtain open so that we can see behind the scene and know that there are evil spirits who want to deflect us from our commitment to Jesus Christ.

Every Christian goes through this sifting process, not just those who experience some of the more obvious trials such as illness, loss of a job, or persecution on the job or in the classroom. If you have ever been tempted, and all of us have, you should know that Satan not only desires to have you, but he has already made meticulous plans for your downfall. It is as though he were sitting there, coiled up and ready to spring up and get you to fall so that all who are watching will think there is little substance to your commitment to Jesus Christ.

So today, as He did to Peter, Jesus is saying, "Satan has asked permission, and it has been granted, just as in the case of Job, to test you. When the temptation is over, I pray that your faith will not fail. And when you are converted, strengthen your brethren. Do not let the regret over your failure destroy you and your witness, but remember that I have prayed for you." Right now, Jesus is before God as your High Priest and remembers you to the Father.

The fact that Jesus has prayed for us and is interceding for us right now is great news when you are experiencing regret. There is, however, more good news—*Jesus knows exactly who we are.*

Remember when Jesus said to Peter, "The cock will not crow today until you have denied three times that you know Me" (Luke 22:34)? Did He say that merely to prove His omniscience? No, the significance to Peter and to us goes far beyond that. The statement revealed that Jesus knew both the circumstances Peter would get into and Peter's weakness.

Consider what Jesus said. He clearly identified the circumstances in which Peter would deny Him. I am convinced He knew precisely where Peter would be seated. He knew that the servant girl would come along and accuse Peter of belonging to Jesus. Incredibly, He knew there would be a rooster in the area who would crow just at the right time to alert Peter to his sin. The Bible report reveals that while Peter was still speaking, the rooster began crowing—perfect timing.

God knows the circumstances that led to your temptation, to your sin, to your failure as a human being. He has accurate knowledge of every temptation, every struggle, every dilemma that you encounter. That is why He can deal with your regret as well.

Jesus knew Peter's weakness, and He knows your weakness. In effect, He said to Peter, "Peter, when you get the chance to say yes to Me and testify for Me, you are going to say no. You are going to be scared to death to identify yourself with Me. Even though outwardly you have often put on a good show, I know how weak you are inside."

Why did Jesus tell Peter that? He wanted to make it easy for Peter to come back to Him. He wanted Peter to know that the hidden weakness revealed during the temptation was no surprise to Him. And He wants us to know it.

A student came to me one day and said, "Oh, I can't face God about this sin again. I can't even face God about my weakness." She thought that possibly God would be shocked. I suggested that He would be disappointed, but He is never caught off guard about our weakness. In fact, Jesus knows things about you that you have not even admitted to yourself. You would not want to know the potential for wickedness in your heart, but God knows. That is why He is able to help you cope with regret.

We have established that you can cope with regret because Jesus prayed for you and Jesus knows your circumstances and weakness. There is a third facet of Peter's experience that is of great value when you are weighed down with regret. *Jesus had compassion for Peter, and He has the same compassion for you.*

If you have experienced any depth of regret, you will have some idea of the torture Peter must have gone through for the three days after the crucifixion of Jesus. Round and round in his head whirled thoughts like, *My last chance to prove my loyalty. My opportunity to confirm my allegiance, and I deny Him. Not once, not twice, but three times! Lord, why did I do it? I'll never be able to forgive myself as long as I live.*

If someone had asked Peter during that time, "Are you a disciple of Jesus?," he may very well have said, "I was once, but I am no longer worthy of that high honor. I've struck out, and I know I'm not going to be included in any future accounting of the twelve disciples of Jesus. His book on me is closed."

Yet that is not the way Jesus treated Peter. Take a look at Mark 16:7. Jesus, speaking to the women who had come to the tomb, said, "But go, tell His disciples *and Peter*" (emphasis added). Just put yourself in the place of those women and imagine what was going on in their minds at that moment. I suspect they were so overwhelmed by the reality of Jesus' resurrection that the final phrase, "and Peter," didn't register too clearly. If it did, they must have wondered about the great compassion of Jesus, clearly forgiving the one who had denied

Him three times. That compassion is, however, totally typical of Jesus.

I trust the women gave Peter Jesus' message. Even if they did not, Jesus' compassion is demonstrated by another phrase in the gospel of Luke. In chapter 24, we read the story of the two disciples who were walking to Emmaus when they were joined by Jesus. After Luke described the whole dramatic incident, he recorded their return to Jerusalem, where they were told, "The Lord has really risen, and has appeared to Simon" (v. 34). In 1 Corinthians 15, the apostle Paul listed the appearances of Jesus after His resurrection, putting the appearance to Peter (Cephas) at the head of the list, indicating Peter was the first to see Jesus. That incident clearly demonstrated that Peter did not need to live with regret anymore. A compassionate Jesus had forgiven him.

Imagine the scene. Jesus puts His arms around Peter, looks in his eyes, and says, "Peter, you fell, but you are not down. You have denied Me, but I am not finished with you yet. You have sinned, but you wept tears of repentance and you are forgiven. I love you, Peter."

I want to remind you that the arms of Jesus even now are reaching out to you in your regret. They are long enough and gentle enough to embrace even the most wayward, backslidden person who has denied the Savior by life and by word. Jesus has His eyes fastened on you, and He says, "I have compassion on you. I will go out of My way to assure you that you can come back into fellowship with the living God."

There is a fourth essential truth if we are to deal effectively with regret, and this is illustrated in John 21:15-17. Jesus is described as having an especially tender moment with Peter. It is the last stage in the restoration of Peter. In one of the most tender scenes in the Bible,

Jesus asked Peter, "Simon, son of John, do you love Me more than these?" (v. 15). Peter responded with a different word for love, brotherly love, instead of the self-giving, agape, love Jesus asked about. Jesus then showed He understood by saying, "Tend My lambs." "OK," Jesus was saying, "You may not feel ready for heavy-duty action yet, but you can start by looking after the lambs in God's flock."

The ever present Jesus then repeated the question, again asking if Peter had that true agape love for Him. Peter was not yet sure of his own heart, so he responded, "Yes, I love You, but with a brotherly love." Jesus replied, "Shepherd My sheep." In effect He said, "I know where you are coming from, but I am sure you can handle more than the lambs."

I don't know how much time elapsed, but a third time Jesus asked, "Do you love me with a phileo (brotherly) love?" Peter was grieved, disturbed that his commitment of brotherly love was not enough, but he repeated his affirmation of love for the third time. Jesus accepted it and said, "Tend My sheep." In effect He said, "I know you are not sure of yourself yet, but I know I can trust you to be a shepherd to God's sheep. Don't let your regret hold you back from the high calling I have given you."

With these new responsibilities, Jesus had restored Peter to his former position of leadership. Regret was replaced by responsibility, indicating full acceptance. Three denials were followed by three affirmations of love and a growing responsibility.

Let's go back to the prayer of Jesus for Peter. Just because Jesus prayed for Peter did not mean that he could not fail. Christ's prayer did not prevent Peter from launching into an impassioned denial of Jesus Christ. But Jesus had said that He was praying for Peter so that "your faith will not fail" in spite of the sin. "Peter," Jesus was saying, "when you have repented and have come back into fellowship with Me, then you can go ahead and feed My sheep."

You would not expect much strength from someone like Peter, would you? Yet sometimes those who have fallen the most, who have been the most overt in their denial of Christ, are the most effective in strengthening the feet of those who have fallen. Think of Peter preaching that great sermon on Pentecost. Read the fantastic encouragement in both 1 and 2 Peter as proof of that.

We have drawn our lessons from only one person who was sifted by Satan during the time preceding the crucifixion. Yet there were two others. One was Christ Himself, sifted by Satan as He prayed in the Garden of Gethsemane. Many think Satan actually tried to kill Jesus there because of the great agony of spirit that He experienced. Yet Jesus turned out to be pure wheat.

Judas was the other person sifted by Satan. Remember how he kissed Jesus on the cheek, yet he denied the Lord for the sake of money. Judas was so filled with remorse that he went and hanged himself. He was sifted by Satan and revealed to be pure chaff.

Peter, like most of us, turned out to be part chaff and part wheat. The process of sifting was one of God's ways of separating the chaff from the wheat. As Peter saw his helplessness and learned to depend on the Holy Spirit, he became a completely different person.

Outwardly, Peter and Judas did essentially the same thing. Both were then filled with regret. Judas, instead of responding to the Savior, let the regret and remorse overwhelm him. He is like the many who, because of financial reverses, because of personal problems in the family, or because they failed themselves and their families, close the ledger by taking their own lives. They live in hell with that regret, for it is regret that helps to make hell truly hell.

Peter, on the other hand, responded to the look of the Savior. He moved closer to the Master through regret instead of away from Him. If you let the Holy Spirit do that while you are experiencing intense regret, He will restore you whether you are in your teens, twenties, thirties, or even nineties. Jesus Christ will then recommission you and say, "OK, now strengthen others."

How do you move from regret to restoration? Accept the fact that Jesus has prayed for you and is now praying for you. Remember that He knows you through and through—and every circumstance you are in. Let His compassion flow out to you and embrace you in forgiving love as you honestly repent of what you have done. Relax in His total acceptance of you, no matter what happened to you or how you sinned. Finally, know that He has restored you to fellowship and new responsibilities. You'll be surprised at how beautifully God will direct you in the future if you let Him forgive the regrets of the past.

Suggested Application

1. List the experiences, the words, and the actions you have taken that still arouse feelings of regret. If they come to mind readily, they are still clearly troublesome.

2. Examine some of the Bible's examples of actions and words that must have brought on feelings of regret. Examples: Reuben (Gen. 37 and 45, particularly vv. 5-8); David (2 Sam. 11, compared to Psalm 51; also 2 Sam. 24).

3. What are the three steps in each example?

4. What can we learn from Psalm 32 about handling the regret that comes with sin?

5. What is the catalog of activity that caused Paul regret (1 Tim. 1:13)? How could he overcome the regret he felt (1 Tim. 1:13-16)?

6. Now consider the answers you gave in number 1 in the light of David's prayers in Psalms 32 and 51 and Paul's statements in 1 Timothy 1:13-16.

11

Tackling the Bitter, Unforgiving Feeling

OUTSIDE, the autumn leaves spilled color across the rolling countryside. Inside, the mood was anything but bright as Karen settled into the pillows for a sleep-inducing chapter of her book. A quick glance at the chapter heading only increased the gloom. The last thing she wanted to read about was "Forgive Us Our Sins . . . As We Forgive Those Who Sin Against Us." She flung the book into the corner of the room and turned on her side to go to sleep.

She had every right to be bitter and unforgiving, she told herself as she lay awake that night. Her best friend from junior high days had refused all social contact with her for the past two years. Though Karen had repeatedly tried to bridge the gap, her friend had maintained her distance. Annoyance had grown into resentment, and resentment into anger. Yes, of course Karen was bitter, but didn't she have a right to be?

Karen's feelings are all too common, even among Christians. There is Bill, who feels that his boss is out to make life miserable for him. He seems to criticize everything Bill does and demeans him in front of the rest of the employees. After three years of this treatment, Bill is ready to explode, and a few days later, he does!

Doris knows all about feelings of anger and bitterness

developing into a hard, unforgiving spirit. She was physically abused by a weak father who beat his children because of his anger at the world. Her mother retreated to hidden caches of wine, leaving Doris in charge of cleaning the house and doing the laundry by the time she was ten. Even though her parents are both dead, she has not yet forgiven them.

Then there is Steve, the once-effective youth leader. One fall he began an innovative program involving parents. Although the program got off to a great start, there were soon whispers of criticism about the parents Steve had chosen. The church gossips got on the phone to line up support against him. Hardliners called the youth leader at home, accusing him of undermining the values of the young people through permitting these parents to participate in supervisory roles. They cornered him in the lobby of the church. Within three months, Steve had to leave the youth program and the church, totally confused by the suddenness of the attack. His head told him that the Lord would vindicate him, but his feelings told him he had been wronged. *I have every right to be bitter,* he thought. *Christians should not behave as the whisperers have—that is clear from Scripture!*

Perhaps the most excruciating experience of bitterness I know is the case of a husband who left town with his two small children, never to be seen again. His wife was left utterly alone in her anguish, fearful that she would never see her children again. Who can comprehend the anguish? Who would not understand if she began carrying a heavy load of bitterness toward her unfeeling husband?

Every one of us has known such feelings of hurt, anger, and bitterness at one time or another. We knew we ought to forgive, but either we could not get ourselves to do it or we did not want to. Nursing feelings of bitterness can be very satisfying as a form of revenge.

Being a Christian, or even having a position of leadership in the church, does not exempt us. For example, consider the disciples of Christ. Did they have the kinds of differences that led to resentment and anger? Yes, they did, for even after being with the Lord Jesus Christ for more than three years, they were still arguing over who would be the greatest in the Kingdom.

I can imagine that Matthew was bothered by Peter because he talked too much. James may have resented his brother John, for John makes it quite clear that he was the disciple Jesus loved. In fact, there may have been others who resented this obvious favorite of Jesus. Or think of Philip, who may well have been embarrassed by Andrew's habit of talking about Jesus to everyone he met. He was forever missing the bus to the next meeting because he was tied up with someone! The disciples were human, and there were undoubtedly disagreements as they lived together as disciples of Christ. Struggles for position, tensions over priorities (such as when the children came to Jesus with their mothers), and personality conflicts are reported in the Bible. Jesus was aware of these. In fact, it is clear that some of His teaching was designed to deal with those feelings of His followers.

When considering the importance of forgiveness, most of us turn to Matthew 18:21. Yet the opening word, "Then," indicates that Peter's question, "Lord, how often shall my brother sin against me and I forgive him?" was triggered by the previous discussion. Notice verse 15: "And if your brother sins, go and reprove him in private; if he listens to you, you have won your brother." The following verses expand on this theme, revealing the pattern for restoring an erring brother or sister. In verse 21, Peter seems to have wondered out loud what to do when a brother refused to be restored despite the loving encouragement of other Christians. He appears not to have noticed that Jesus' focus was not on the one sinned against but on the sinning one.

When the Holy Spirit approaches us about our need to forgive someone who has sinned against us, we are usually more concerned about our feelings. We tend to focus on *our* need to forgive, on overcoming *our* bitterness and anger. The whole exercise and experience of forgiving someone else is designed, we are convinced, solely to help us feel better.

But by implication, Jesus in Matthew 18:15 taught that this focus on our feelings is wrong. The goal is not to get us straightened out; it is to restore the brother or sister to fellowship. We are not to be so much concerned about our clear conscience as we are about the restoration into fellowship of the person who has sinned against us. In other words, the goal of forgiveness is restoration.

The simple fact is that when we become truly concerned about the broken relationship with our brother or sister, we will become more concerned about them than we are about ourselves. When that happens, the anger and bitterness and the unforgiving spirit are naturally dissolved in our concern for the other person. This is particularly true when we do exactly what Jesus tells us to do: "Go and reprove him in private." There is no way you can maintain your anger, bitterness, and unforgiving spirit as you meet in private with your "enemy," with restoration to fellowship as the goal.

Unfortunately, most of us have never read Jesus' procedure for restoring the person who has sinned—or we disregard it. We much prefer to get on the telephone and voice a prayer concern about someone who has sinned (especially if it is against us and our sensibilities). Or we express our concern at prayer meeting, for we are sure that the sanctuary will sanctify our gossip. Or else we use prayers as a substitute for obedience, for going "in private" to the person who has sinned.

"But," you say, "I know I can forgive. I can even welcome that person into my circle of fellowship, but I cannot and will not *forget*. Don't get me involved in any project that would force me to work closely with that person, for I do not want to get hurt again. I want to protect myself from repeatedly getting hurt."

Beware of that attitude. That is not biblical forgiveness. True biblical forgiveness says, "I am willing to restore, to gain, to win my brother and sister." You see, that is the way God treated us when we came to Him in repentance and faith. He forgave us our sin and said, "I will remember it no more."

At this point I can imagine what you are thinking. You are thinking, *OK, I'll grant you that the goal of forgiveness is reconciliation. But do you understand what that is going to cost me?*

Yes, I do, for Jesus illustrated that as well in Matthew 18:23-35. Peter asked, "Lord, how often shall my brother sin against me and I forgive him? Up to seven times?" I sense that Peter in that question was trying to deal with restoring the sinning brother or sister. And in his mind he was saying, *Lord, you are really letting those sinning people get off easily. I go to the person who has wronged me, show him his sin in love and forgiveness, and he promptly admits his sin. I know human nature, and it won't be long and he will wrong me again. So I go back and am able to restore him again. Off he goes on his way—and two weeks later he has cheated me again. How long can this go on?*

The rabbis had taught that you forgive a person three times. Peter went for the biblical number, seven. He expected to be congratulated for his magnanimity. So when Jesus said, "I do not say to you, up to seven times," Peter was thinking, *See, I was too high*. He could not believe his ears when Jesus continued, "but up to seventy times seven" (18:22). Peter's mental calculator lit up and numbers started flashing, settling on 490. Mind-boggling! You might as well say "a zillion times." For in reality, Jesus was saying that forgiveness must be unlimited.

To help Peter and the others present understand the cost of this kind of forgiveness, Jesus told the parable of the wealthy king who had his annual accounting of receivables, of debts owed him. In the lineup was an absolutely terrified debtor who would rather face an angry wife than the king, for his debt had become so large that he could not possibly repay it. The king looked at the sum the man owed him and thundered, in effect, "You scoundrel. You've taken advantage of my generosity long enough." Turning to his treasurer, he said, "Sell him, his wife, and his children on the slave market. We'll get what we can. At least then his debt won't rise next year."

The man thought of his lovely wife and beautiful children and threw himself at the feet of the king, saying, "I realize I have not done right by you. Give me some time and I really will repay everything I owe you."

The king looked down at the groveling debtor for a long minute and then said, "I ought to have my head examined, but I will let you go free this time. You will not need to go to auction on the slave market. I am forgiving you all your indebtedness for the sake of your wife and children."

I suspect the man did not even stop for a cup of coffee on his way home. He burst into the house and shouted, "We're free! The king has forgiven us all our indebtedness. We are free!" He may even have gone on to the neighbors to tell of the king's generosity.

Jesus told this story for the sake of Peter and the disciples—and all those who would some day read it in the Bible. The wealthy king is God. We have, in effect, all stood before His judgment bar and heard God say, "You owe me an infinite amount of righteousness, for that is what I require of man." And not one of us could pay it. No matter how hard we try, we will not impress God with our goodness. So God, through the death of Jesus Christ, freely forgave us our sin.

The king freely forgave his debtor, just as God has freely forgiven us. That makes forgiveness free, does it not? Wrong. Forgiveness is never free. True, from the standpoint of the debtor, the forgiveness of his debt was free. From our standpoint as believers, the forgiveness of our sin was free. In both cases, however, the cost was great. Let it be written in mile-high letters: *The cost of forgiveness is great. The cost of reconciliation is immeasurable.*

In the parable, the king absorbed the cost. He had to make a huge bad-debt entry, a ten-million-dollar write-off in today's dollars. It cost him a major chunk of his fortune to forgive the debtor.

Even so, God gives forgiveness freely to repentant sinners, but that does not make it cheap. God absorbed the debt of our sin when Jesus died on the cross in our place. He payed His own justice its due.

How does this apply when we forgive one another? The point to remember is that the score always has to be evened. Here's a man who commits adultery and his wife forgives him. How is that score evened? She absorbs the loss when she forgives her husband. The one who is sinned against bears in her own body, in her emotions and spirit, the brunt of the sin committed against her. Because that is the case, she has the right and the ability to do as the king did, forgive.

Is that right? Let me ask you another question. Is it right that Jesus Christ died on the cross, taking in His own body the penalty for our sin, the penalty we deserved? Paul spoke to that when he wrote, "And be kind one to another, tender-hearted, forgiving each other, just as God in Christ also has forgiven you" (Eph. 4:32). Once we see that our standard of forgiveness is set by the forgiveness Jesus extended to us by dying in our place, we can understand why we must forgive our brother or sister so many times. We recognize that the debt is paid through the hurt we bear when we forgive the other person freely—just as Christ forgave us.

But, you say, "I just am not ready to bear that cost. There is too much at stake now. I will forgive later when I am in a better position emotionally to bear the cost." Take another look at the cost of unforgiveness in Jesus' parable. Notice that the debtor who had been completely forgiven went out after he had finished his rejoicing and demanded instant payment from someone who owed him a small amount. It was the size of debt you might owe a friend because your money ran out on a trip and you borrowed a twenty-dollar bill. Instead of having mercy on his debtor, the forgiven man threw his friend in prison until he could pay back the twenty dollars he owed.

In those days there was no legal aid, so the man in prison was without recourse at law. Nor did the police permit him the one mandatory telephone call U.S. law demands. His friends had to take action on his behalf (Fortunate the man who has friends like that!); they notified the king of this ungrateful act. The king then summoned the man whom he had previously forgiven and asked: "You wicked slave, I forgave you all that debt because you entreated me. Should you not also have had mercy on your fellow slave, even as I had mercy on you?" (Matt. 18:32-33). And the king handed the man over to the torturers until he would repay that which he had once been forgiven!

End of story? No, for Jesus then emphasized the cost of bitterness, anger, and an *unforgiving* spirit by saying, "So shall My heavenly Father also do to you, if each of you does not forgive his brother from your heart" (v. 35).

Let's be specific. You may go to church Sunday morning, knowing you have not given God the time He deserved during the week. It is communion Sunday and you know you cannot take the bread and the cup with that between you and God. So you confess it and are forgiven. Then as you walk toward your car, you see a business associate who took advantage of your absence during vacation to ingratiate himself with the boss. You start telling your family about it for the hundredth time and say, "I hope God gets him for that!"

What is the cost of your unforgiveness? The immediate cost may be the loss of respect in your family (usually not expressed, but it happens just the same). Another cost is personal stress. The real cost is that expressed by Jesus: "So shall My heavenly Father also do to you, if each of you does not forgive his brother from your heart." We should not interpret this verse to mean that God revokes our forgiveness if we don't forgive others, but He does promise us torment if we withhold forgiveness from *anyone* who has wronged us.

Years ago my pastor's wife made a statement that is so true here: "Forgiveness is something good that you do for yourself." In other words, forgiving someone else has the benefit of restoring that person, but you benefit as well, because if you maintain that bitterness it will cloud your spirit and your relationships with everyone around you—and you will be cast into the emotional torture that is inevitable if you do not forgive.

You say, "OK, I recognize that the goal of forgiveness is reconciliation. I am aware of the cost to God of forgiving me my sin, and I know what it will cost me if I forgive the person who has wronged me. I'll admit as well the emotional cost of unforgiveness. But how do I get myself to forgive? I don't feel a bit like forgiving anyone."

That last sentence is at the root of most unforgiving attitudes. We have been taught that our feelings are important, that they are the motivators to action. If we do not *feel* like doing something, we should not do it. Some go so far as to say that until you feel like doing it, the Holy Spirit is not guiding you.

Take another look at verse 35 of Matthew 18. Then go back and read verses 21 and 22. Do you find anything about the need to *feel* like forgiving anyone? Jesus clearly and unequivocally gave a command. We are to forgive our brother or sister an unlimited number of times, *no matter how little we feel like doing it.* Amazingly, feelings always follow obedience, even if they may lag a bit because our emotional makeup is sluggish.

You may be one of those who has been rejected by your parents. In your heart you are saying, and you may well be saying it to your spouse, "I want to see my parents suffer for what they have done to me. No way am I going to let them off scot-free by forgiving them." You say that even though in your most honest hours, you admit they couldn't care less about whether you forgave them or not. They have rejected you—and they will continue to reject you. Your clear response, if you want to live by God's Word, must be, "By God's grace I choose to forgive them. I choose to forgive them for all the hurt they have caused me." That will, I can assure you, take you out of the torture chamber of bitterness, anger, and resentment.

Why do I say that? I say it not only because I know it is psychologically sound, but because it is biblically sound as well. Christ taught that we have the power to bind anything on earth or loose it; He said that if two of us agree on earth about anything, it shall be done; and these promises apply directly to the act of reconciliation and forgiveness. Special help is available when we forgive another and when believers are reconciled. That's why those promises appear right in the middle of Christ's discussion of forgiveness (Matt. 18:18-20).

There are marriages across this land that are bound because there has been no loving confrontation and reconciliation. There are families in which the Spirit of God is not free to work because of unforgiving attitudes. Churches are bound, unable to glorify God, because of irreconcilable factions in the church. The Lord wants to loose you and me through honest, loving confrontation, forgiveness, and restoration.

Some years ago a revival swept through western Canada and into parts of the United States. One of the events that sparked it happened in a Baptist church in Saskatoon, Saskatchewan. In that church, two brothers had not spoken to each other for thirteen years. They would enter and leave the church sanctuary through different doors. Both had long ago given up on prayer. The pastor, who was one of the few who knew about the feud, said to them during the early days of the revival in that church, "I'm going to bring both of you down to the basement, and we as deacons are going to gather around you. We are not letting you go until you are reconciled. Take as much time as you want, but we are going to be praying and asking God to bring peace into this situation."

So the pressure was on. Finally, one brother said to the other, "OK, I want you to forgive me for all the wrong that I've done."

And the other responded, "Well, it's about time. It's about time you see that you are at fault in this whole business."

The pastor and the deacons just kept on praying. Others joined in as the deacons said, "God, this isn't good enough. We've got to get a genuine reconciliation." Well, the Holy Spirit of God came into that circle and took those two men apart, piece by piece. One of the people in the auditorium said he heard the man with the haughty spirit eventually pound the downstairs wall for twenty minutes, asking God to forgive him, repenting of the bitterness that had been built up in him. The next evening, those two brothers sang a duet in that church. It was from that atmosphere, that kind of loosing of bound spirits, that the revival spread through hundreds of churches. All over the land, believers met in loving confrontation as families were reconciled, pegple in churches were reconciled, and the many hurts of life were healed.

How do you tackle a bitter, unforgiving spirit within you? You go in obedience to Christ, regardless of how you feel, and tell the one who has hurt you that you forgive him or her. You do it by faith in the Christ who died for you and forgave your sin. And if you do not get a response? Then just like Jesus, you wait until that person's heart is opened to your loving forgiveness.

Let's etch the words of Paul on our minds: "And be kind to one another, tender-hearted, forgiving each other, just as God in Christ also has forgiven you" (Eph. 4:32).

If you've got someone to forgive, do it *now*.

Suggested Application

1. Name the one person or organization that you feel most bitter about. List the reasons why you think you have every right to feel bitter.

2. Now list the reasons why God should be displeased with you on the basis of your actions during your adult years.

3. Read what God has done for you in the light of the things listed in number 2 (Rom. 5:1-8; Eph. 1:3-7; 1 Pet. 2:24).

4. How are we to treat those who genuinely mistreat us, according to Jesus (Matt. 5:44)?

5. Consider creative ways in which you can do good to those who have caused the bitterness in your heart. Take the first step today to begin implementing that plan of action.

12

Living with Sorrow

ONE SPRING day, a car with four young people skidded on an icy stretch of pavement in Canada. The eighteen-year-old driver swerved to the opposite ditch, hoping to miss an oncoming truck. But unfortunately, he was only partially successful. His own life was spared, but the two young people in the back seat and a young mother in the front were killed instantly.

One of those young people killed was my nephew, whose name was Dallas. He was my brother's oldest child, his only son. He was the first member of our immediate family to die. Though I had attended scores of funerals in my lifetime, this one was different. Death had struck close to home. Sorrow, that deep sense of pain and loss, became ours by personal experience.

Our world is filled with sorrow. The wife of a friend of mine chose to file for divorce recently. For Joe, his wife's action was as intense as if she had died. If she had died, he would have accepted the loss more easily than he could the divorce. His loneliness was compounded by extreme feelings of regret mixed with generous doses of anger and bitterness. Reading the Bible seemed impossible, prayer futile.

Consider also the sorrow experienced by families who have to move every two or three years because the head office says so. After months of house-hunting, they find exactly the kind of neighborhood in which their children can be raised. The children start off to school, eventually make friends, and develop relationships with the children in the neighborhood. Mother starts volunteer work at the hospital, serves with a women's group at church, and enters into significant relationships with several women. Then the husband is told, "Now if you want a promotion, you will have to move to yet another city." The sorrow that this family experiences from the breakup of relationships can be traumatic for most members, for they know that in all likelihood they will never make contact with their friends again.

Sorrow is not necessarily bad, however. In fact, it can be most beneficial if handled right. It can be God's way of causing us to enter another phase of our life, a time of life that will have its own benefits. Yet improperly handled, sorrow can be devastating. Sorrow can lock people into a total preoccupation with past relationships and events and thus prevent growth.

Think of the widow of a well-liked professor who had built up a considerable library. Determined to maintain the memory of her late husband, the widow insists that his library be left intact. No one can come to use the books, nor can they be given away. That would be disloyal to the memory of her husband. As a result, she never re-enters life the way God expects her to; she stays home, bogged down with memories.

Then there is the person loaded down with a tremendous amount of guilt. He takes responsibility for things that may have contributed to the death of a loved one. I remember visiting the home of a widow whose husband had died of a heart attack years ago. Over and over she said, "If he had only been persuaded to see a doctor. I told him he ought to go, but maybe if I had been more persistent he would have gone." That kind of guilt leads to a neurotic preoccupation with "if only" and is not pleasing to God. As human beings, we are subject to all kinds of frailties and we make many mistakes, but God does not expect us to live with the guilt caused by our weaknesses. We are not omniscient; only God is.

I believe that we can learn how to mourn in a profitable way, how to re-enter life after tragedy, from the life of Jesus Christ. His example gives us clues to how we can and should respond to sorrow. Isaiah told us that He was "a man of sorrows and acquainted with grief," so we will examine several situations in which grief touched Him.

As I considered Jesus' response to tragedy, I asked myself the question, "How did Jesus respond when His cousin, John the Baptist, was brutally murdered?" Their mothers had been good friends, so there is reason to believe that John and Jesus knew each other well before that public baptism at Jordan. Now this preacher of righteousness, the forerunner of the Messiah, had fallen victim to the vicious hatred of Herod's wife, Herodias. At the request of this woman's daughter, John the Baptist's head had been carried in on a platter in a gruesome display of vindictiveness.

Matthew reported that "his disciples came and took away the body and buried it; and they went and reported to Jesus" (Matt. 14:12). His reaction is reported in verse 13: "Now when Jesus heard it, He withdrew from there in a boat, to a lonely place by Himself." Jesus' action illustrates the first principle in living with sorrow: *He withdrew to a lonely place.* True, He later requested the help of His friends, but for the time being He needed to be alone.

Like Jesus, there are times when our thoughts are so private, our sorrow so intense and we hurt so much, that we need to get alone with God and pour out our complaints to Him. For one thing, we need to get alone to meditate. A time of sorrow presents an opportunity to reflect upon the past, to evaluate our lives, to distinguish what is important from what is unimportant. At such a time we begin to ask, "God, as I consider my frailty, what do You want me to do?" This time of meditation can lead to significant new beginnings if we do not stay with the past.

Furthermore, I think those times alone should be spent in prayer. That is actually what Jesus intended to do, but the multitudes heard of His retreat and barged in on Him. In fact, their presence led directly to the feeding of the five thousand. But when that was over, "immediately He made the disciples get into the boat, and go ahead of Him to the other side. . . . And after He had sent the multitudes away, He went up to the mountain by Himself to pray; and when it was evening, He was there alone" (Matt. 14:22-23).

It is in the quietness of our souls that we ought to pour out our hearts before God. There may be times when we are upset and even angry, but we ought to be honest with the Lord God. Read the story of David in Psalm 77. In effect David was saying, "I pour out my complaint to You, God. Is it going to be this way forever? Are You never going to listen to me? Are You never going to be concerned about me again?" In words like that, David unleashed the agony of his spirit before God. Today we also need times like that when we are honest with God, when we pour out our frustrations and desires in our sorrow.

Yet Jesus did not stay alone. He kept life in balance, as we need to, and resumed normal activities. He went from a time alone to feeding the five thousand. Then, after another time alone He went to the disciples, walking to them on the water as they were afraid of capsizing in the storm. He went from His need to their need. That is the second principle: *We must resume the normal activities of life.*

You and I have both seen instances when after a funeral, loved ones and friends come in and do everything for the grieving survivor. "Now just lie down; we want you to do nothing," they may say to the mother who has lost a son. "We will scrub your floors, do your dishes." Yet this expression of Christian love poses a problem, if overdone. The person beset by sorrow may develop an unrealistic picture of life and may have difficulty re-entering life to make those common, everyday decisions so necessary to living with your sorrow.

One of the most important things you can do in a time of sorrow is to continue, as much as possible, the normal activities that force you to make decisions. This will help you to orient yourself to your new life without the loved one. Even if you do not have to go to work on a job, it is important to keep up activities at home that will move you forward. Inactivity lets you dwell too much on the tragedy. That's why Jesus resumed His regular schedule.

The story of David in the Old Testament contains a striking example illustrating this principle. When Absalom his son had been killed by Joab after an intense battle won by David's army, David went to an upper chamber and wept. Hadn't he given the command that Absalom's life was to be spared despite his rebellion? Now he was dead, and David was overcome with grief.

When Joab was told, "Behold, the king is weeping and mourns for Absalom" (2 Sam. 19:1), he went to David and said in effect, "David, don't you realize that your mourning is going to create real problems for you? The people have won a great victory, and you are overcome by sorrow. If you don't snap out of it and join the victory celebrations, the soldiers will go home. Your mourning is simply unrealistic in the light of what was accomplished by your people." Though David was personally deeply grieved by the death of his son, he needed to re-enter life and resume his normal kingly duties if he was to hold the respect of his people.

Just as David needed to think of others in his grief, so one of the best ways to cope with sorrow is to begin to think of the needs of others. Jesus also provides us with an example in John 13. He knew He was about to die, and already this must have caused some inner heaviness. Yet He rose from supper, took a towel, and poured water to start washing the disciples' feet. Even though He knew what was coming, He thought of others. Nothing will help you overcome sorrow like asking, "How can I get involved in the needs of others?" The moment you start thinking and acting like that, you will discover people with far greater needs than yours. I can personally testify to this, that no matter how tragic your situation may be, there are situations even more tragic. This helps to provide balance to our experience and makes it easier to live with sorrow.

A third principle that I find in the life of Christ is that *there is a time to mourn and a time to be joyful.* The disciples of John came to Jesus and asked, "Why do we and the Pharisees fast, but Your disciples do not fast?" (Matt. 9:14). And Jesus said in reply that while the Bridegroom is present, it is time to rejoice, but when He is absent they will mourn. And in John 16:20-21 Jesus said, "You will weep and lament, but the world will rejoice; you will be sorrowful, but your sorrow will be turned to joy. Whenever a woman is in travail she has sorrow, because her hour has come; but when she gives birth to the child, she remembers the anguish no more, for joy that a child has been born into the world." Jesus was in effect reiterating what Ecclesiastes says: There is a time to mourn, but there also is a time to laugh (Eccles. 3:4). In other words, everything has its time—and sorrow has its time, too.

We could with profit reinstate an Old Testament practice, that of a certain period of mourning for the dead. It was an excellent idea from the psychological viewpoint. For forty days after a person died, his family would mourn, and then life resumed its normal pattern. In no way do I suggest that you can forget the loved one in forty days. You cannot and you never will. But it does mean that you realize that it is unrealistic to spend your whole life in mourning. There is a time to mourn, but there is also a time to rejoice.

Years ago in Europe and in some ethnic communities in the United States, people used to wear black armbands for perhaps three months after a loved one died. This was a sign that the members of the family were going through mourning. I think that was a healthy thing to do—to recognize that there are times when we mourn and there are times when we rejoice, to see it as a phase of life rather than the normal experience for the rest of life. Then mourning becomes a period of development and change rather than an endless process that we take with us to the grave.

Another principle Jesus exemplified during a period of sorrow is that *He requested the help of friends.* This time we see Jesus in Gethsemane. He had come to the garden with His disciples and asked them to pray for Him. He took Peter, James, and John with Him and "began to be grieved and distressed" (Matt. 26:37). I don't know how much of this was visible to the three disciples, but they certainly should have understood the implicit call for help when He said to them, "My soul is deeply grieved, to the point of death; remain here and keep watch with Me" (v. 38).

The amazing thing is that although the disciples were not very good at encouraging the Lord in His final night of agony, He did not consider it beneath His dignity to ask for their help and prayer support. Sometimes we think that someone as strong as Jesus, or a friend we know, really does not need that support. But Jesus did. And if Jesus needed it, how much more do we in our hour of grief?

You say, "I don't have close friends like that." Then call someone you do not know as well. He may well become your closest friend as a result of joining in your sorrow in prayer. Simply say to that person, "I am going to ask you to stand with me during this time of personal grief. I want you to pray with me, and for me, and uphold me in a ministry of encouragement during this time." God gives us friends for times like this; that's what the Body of Christ, the local church, is all about.

I see a fifth principle in the life of Jesus. *He accepted tragedy as the will of God.* We read, "The Son of Man is to go, just as it is written of Him" (Matt. 26:24). Jesus was saying that His death was not an accident. It was part of a divine plan, and He accepted it as such. They could not take Him until His hour was come.

We, too, must accept tragedy as part of the divine plan. We are continually saying, "What *if* we had called the doctor sooner. *If* he had operated, the person would have lived." We get so bogged down in the "what ifs" of life because we have never really accepted the tragedy as part of the divine plan. And one of the reasons is that we act as if life depends on us, as if it is our responsibility if someone dies. Yet if we are acting on the basis of information available to us and somehow make a wrong decision, we must accept our loved one's death as the will of God. If not, we become overloaded with guilt and may be crippled for the rest of our lives.

Consider this fact: Jesus, as the Son of God, could have prevented the death of John the Baptist. He could have spoken the word, and John would have lived and Herod died instead. Jesus had all that power in His fingers, by the word of His mouth. He didn't use it, yet He did not live with guilt, either, or a neurotic preoccupation with the tragic death of His cousin. He accepted the total picture as the will of God. John the Baptist's death was as much a part of God's plan as was the death of Christ.

There are cases of reasonable guilt. You may have had a bad relationship with the person who died. You may have mistreated that person. If so, you must realize that there is forgiveness for your sin. We read in 1 John 1 :9: "If we confess our sins, He is faithful and righteous to forgive us our sins and to cleanse us from all unrighteousness." That commitment by God includes all of those wrong decisions, misjudgments, and sins in your life. God wants you to be free so that you might have confidence toward Him, so that you might bow humbly and accept the situation as from His hand even though you bear responsibility. When you confess it, it is blotted out as far as your relationship with God is concerned. God wants you to be released from guilt through His forgiveness.

Notice also that *Christ bore no resentment*. When Jesus was on the cross, He said, "Father, forgive them; for they do not know what they are doing" (Luke 23:34). That's the sixth lesson we can learn from Him. We need to be reminded of this because at no time are we more critical than at the time of a tragedy. I pity doctors.

When a patient dies, they get blamed for having operated, and if they did not operate, they get blamed for that. We sometimes expect the medical profession to play God, to know precisely how the treatment is going to work out. If it does not work out the way we think it should, we hold them accountable. We get very critical of anyone and anything associated with the death of a loved one.

Jesus could have been critical, too. He could have said, "I have done no wrong; I am sinless." He could have thought to Himself, *Why is it that I am being unjustly punished and bearing the sins of the world? On top of that, I am being accused of things I didn't do.* Yet Jesus bore no resentment. He died with a spirit free of anger, hatred, or retaliation.

Jesus gave us a clue to what our attitude is to be toward sorrow when in the Sermon on the Mount He said, "Blessed are those who mourn, for they shall be comforted" (Matt. 5:4). As we accept our grief, our sorrow can be used of God to develop within us the ability to comfort others.

When I flew to Canada for the funeral of my nephew, my brother and I discussed all the "ifs" by which the accident might have been avoided. If only they had been going a little slower, if only they had started out a little earlier—if, if. You can easily come up with a hundred ifs. But I was so pleased when my brother said to me, "You know, if what you wrote in one of your books was right, it means that we have to accept this as the will of God without all the ifs." And I think that is how God wants us to respond to tragedy.

This does not mean that we do not sorrow. Jesus wept openly at the grave of Lazarus. But as Christians, we must ultimately accept sorrow as part of the fabric of life and not let it cloud the rest of our lives. If we let sorrow tie us to the past, we will never get free and experience life as Jesus wants us to experience it. There is a time to cry, there is a time to dance, there is a time to weep, and there is a time to laugh. We can do it as we respond positively to what God lets enter our lives.

Finally, *Christ believed our sorrow was only temporary.* That's why He told His disciples, "Let not your heart be troubled" (John 14:1). He was leaving to prepare a place for them, "And if I go and prepare a place for you, I will come again, and receive you to Myself; that where I am, there you may be also" (John 14:3). Read the descriptions of heaven in the book of Revelation and you'll be convinced with Paul the apostle that "the sufferings of this present time are not worthy to be compared with the glory that is to be revealed to us" (Rom. 8:18).

Remember that when a believer dies, we do not sorrow for him. In the last analysis, grief is for ourselves. A part of us is gone, but our loved one is with the Lord, which is "far better."

Believers have the assurance that their sorrow will indeed be turned into joy. Christ taught, "Blessed are those who mourn, for they shall be comforted."

Suggested Application

1. Study John 11:1-40 as an example of sorrow. The fact of Christ's special love for Martha, Mary, and Lazarus did not exempt them from heartbreak. Why did Christ wait before returning to Bethany (v. 6)? Why could Christ say He was glad despite the sorrow of the family (v. 15)? What words of comfort did Christ speak to those who mourned (v. 25)? What does Christ's own response tell us about His identification with human need?

2. Read Revelation 21:1-7. How will the emotion of sorrow be resolved in heaven?

3. Discuss: When is sorrow normal and healthy? When does it become abnormal and destructive?

CHRISTIAN HERALD ASSOCIATION AND ITS MINISTRIES

CHRISTIAN HERALD ASSOCIATION, founded in 1878, publishes The Christian Herald Magazine, one of the leading interdenominational religious monthlies in America. Through its wide circulation, it brings inspiring articles and the latest news of religious developments to many families. From the magazine's pages came the initiative for CHRISTIAN HERALD CHILDREN'S HOME and THE BOWERY MISSION, two individually supported not-for-profit corporations.

CHRISTIAN HERALD CHILDREN'S HOME, established in 1894, is the name for a unique and dynamic ministry to disadvantaged children, offering hope and opportunities which would not otherwise be available for reasons of poverty and neglect. The goal is to develop each child's potential and to demonstrate Christian compassion and understanding to children in need.

Mont Lawn is a permanent camp located in Bushkill, Pennsylvania. It is the focal point of a ministry which provides a healthful "vacation with a purpose" to children who without it would be confined to the streets of the city. Up to 1000 children between the ages of 7 and 11 come to Mont Lawn each year.

Christian Herald Children's Home maintains year-round contact with children by means of an *In-City Youth Ministry*. Central to its philosophy is the belief that only through sustained relationships and demonstrated concern can individual lives be truly enriched. Special emphasis is on individual guidance, spiritual and family counseling and tutoring. This follow-up ministry to inner-city children culminates for many in financial assistance toward higher education and career counseling.

THE BOWERY MISSION, located at 227 Bowery, New York City, has since 1879 been reaching out to the lost men on the Bowery, offering them what could be their last chance to rebuild their lives. Every man is fed, clothed and ministered to. Countless numbers have entered the 90-day residential rehabilitation program at the Bowery Mission. A concentrated ministry of counseling, medical care, nutrition therapy, Bible study and Gospel services awakens a man to spiritual renewal within himself.

These ministries are supported solely by the voluntary contributions of individuals and by legacies and bequests. Contributions are tax deductible. Checks should be made out either to CHRISTIAN HERALD CHILDREN'S HOME or to THE BOWERY MISSION.

Administrative Office: 40 Overlook Drive, Chappaqua, New York 10514
Telephone: (914) 769-9000